PELHAM CRAFT SERIES

Papier Mâché Work

TERENCE McLAUGHLIN

PELHAM BOOKS

First published in Great Britain by
PELHAM BOOKS LTD
52 Bedford Square
London, W.C.1
1975
© 1974 by Terence McLaughlin

ISBN 0 7207 0723 4

Filmset in 10/12pt Univers Medium and printed by
BAS Printers Limited, Wallop, Hampshire
and bound by Dorstel Press, Harlow

Contents

Illustrations

INTRODUCTION

What Papier Mâché Is

For most people, I think, papier mâché is associated with two apparently unrelated worlds — one world of nineteenth-century trays and furniture of incredible elegance and complexity, often decorated with pictures of Academy standard, or intricate patterns in gold leaf and mother-of-pearl, and another world of small children at school playing around with great heaps of wet newspaper and producing models that have an uncanny resemblance to great heaps of wet newspaper.

The real world of papier mâché work lies in between these extremes. I cannot tell you how to make articles like the piece in Plate 1, just as I cannot tell you how to paint like Turner or Raphael, but you will find in this book a host of useful, elegant or amusing things to make that have no resemblance to heaps of wet newspaper.

Papier mâché, as its name suggests, is made of mashed paper — paper broken down into small pieces by tearing and soaking, or even into a pulpy mass of fibres by boiling. It is put together again with the addition of glue, paste, or other adhesives, and usually waterproofed with lacquer, varnish or paint. This description is accurate, as far as it goes, but it does not adequately suggest the great versatility and strength of good papier mâché. I find it better to think of the material, not as broken down paper, but as a synthetic material. Paper is, after all, made by breaking down wood to its component fibres and removing the hard and waterproof lignin: papier mâché takes the fibres, shapes them into suitable forms, and restores the strength and water-resistance with adhesives and

varnishes. And the material is almost as hard as wood, and often tougher. Well-made papier mâché can be dropped, sat on, left out in the rain or hit with a hammer, without coming to much harm.

Some idea of the quality of the material may be judged from the papier mâché *houses* made by Charles Frederick Bielefeld, one of the greatest of the nineteenth-century workers in papier mâché. Apparently an emigrant named Seymour, bound for Australia, conceived in 1833 the very far-sighted idea of carrying a prefabricated village with him, to house his party of emigrants until they could build more permanent structures. Bielefeld, always ready to rise to a challenge, constructed a whole collection of buildings, including ten cottages and a ten-roomed villa, in papier mâché. The smaller houses could be taken down or put up in four hours. While they were awaiting shipment, the houses were erected at the railway yard at Staines, on the river Thames west of London, and a sudden flood from the river immersed them in water to a depth of two feet. Such was the quality of the treated paper that the houses were completely unharmed by this soaking, and subsequently got to Australia intact, the first successful enterprise in the manufacture of portable buildings for export.

Even more of an advertisement for the water-resistance of papier mâché is the remarkable feat of Isaac Weld, an Irishman from County Cork, and a great traveller in America — he wrote a book called *Weld's Travels* and was a friend of Presidents Washington and Jefferson. In 1800 Weld made a papier mâché boat and sailed it on the lakes of Killarney: the details of his method have not survived, but he must have been as ingenious in his treatment of the paper as Bielefeld.

The origin of papier mâché is, of course, bound up with the history of paper. The ancient Egyptians, accustomed to handling papyrus reed, turned surplus papyrus documents into papier mâché coffin liners and even whole sarcophagi, gilded to look like the wooden coffins they replaced — evidence that in every civilization, however old, people are always looking for a cheap substitute for conventional materials. The art died out after the Romans virtually took over Egypt, because less papyrus was used. Vellum and parchment became the preferred materials for documents, and although they could be turned into glue when quite useless, parchment sheets were too tough to make a pulp for construction work. Then, when paper started to be used in large quantities again, it seems that the idea of breaking the paper down and reconstituting it into new forms occurred to several groups of people at around the same time.

In China and Japan the technique of waterproofing layers of paper was current around the end of the seventeenth century, and at the same time workers in France were making snuff boxes and other small decorative articles in paper pulp stiffened and waterproofed with copal varnish.

In England, again at the same period, a manufacturer called Wilton, operating from a factory at Charing Cross, London, was turning out large quantities of papier mâché ornaments for sticking to furniture, chimney pieces, doors, and so on, in the elaborate style of the time. His mâché was a mixture of paper pulp, straw, plaster and other materials known as *fibrous slab*. The use of these ornaments to replace plaster ones became even greater in the eighteenth century, and we have records of the supply of ornaments for redecorating a drawing room at Dunster Castle in 1758 — all the ornamentation for a large and richly decorated room was sent down from London (presumably Wilton's factory) in a box weighing only 50 lb., a quarter in weight of the same amount of plaster work.

Painted papier mâché, of the type that is familiar in museums, was invented by John Baskerville around 1740 as an extension of his business in making 'japanned' ware, an imitation of the Japanese lacquered furniture. He pasted sheets of paper together and put them under immense pressure, then painted them with a black durable varnish. Birmingham, where Baskerville worked, became the centre for the production of papier mâché work, and Henry Clay, his apprentice, invented a process for making papier mâché that was hard, water-resistant and virtually heat-proof, and was stronger than wood. Clay's own description says:

"My inventions of making paper panels for various purposes, are by pasting several papers upon boards or plates of regular thicknesses on each side of the same, to prevent one side contracting or drawing with superior force to the other in drying . . . they are rubbed over, or dipped in oil or varnish, which so immediately drenches into them as to secure them from damp, etc. After the papers are thus made they are capable of being sawed into different forms, and planed as wood; and if joining the parts be required, as in tea-trays, dressing-boxes and some articles, they are done by dovetailing or mitring, in the same manner as if made from wood.

"After the various articles are thus formed in the paper, they are coated with colour and oils sufficiently to make the surface even, and are then japanned and highly varnished and can be brought to the highest polish by friction with the human hand."

Clay's raw material was strong rag paper rather like modern blotting paper, used in about ten layers and stuck together with a mixture of glue, flour and resin. His lacquer was a mixture of lampblack, Virginian turpentine, balsam, linseed oil, pitch, resin and wax. The effects of rubbing this shoe-polish sort of compound into trays with 'the human hand' can only be imagined with difficulty, but factory workers were obviously less conscious of factory hygiene in the eighteenth century. The real success of his papier mâché was due to the process of impregnating the paper layers with oil and varnish and heating them to dry the oil, thus making the whole mass of paper fibres entirely waterproof.

After Clay's patent expired, a great many companies were set up to make similar goods. Jennens and Bettridge were the most successful: many of their beautiful pieces of work are still in museums and private collections, and they were well-enough known in their own times to need branches in Birmingham, London, and New York — "Jennens & Bettridge, Makers of Papier-Mâché Goods, at 218 Pearl Street" according to a directory of New York in 1851. The address is very suitable, as this company were the first to exploit the use of mother-of-pearl in decoration of papier mâché work. The natural play of colours over the thin layers of shell was supplemented by clever use of coloured varnish, so that the pieces of shell looked like luminous flower petals on the black ground of the lacquered tray.

Cheaper copies of the Jennens and Bettridge type of tray used roughly cut pieces of shell, supplemented by paint, and often the borders, instead of being actual floral shapes, were simply broken pieces of the shell used in whatever shapes they came.

In America papier mâché was also very popular, and apart from the imported objects there was a flourishing home-produced trade. William Allgood, a Northamptonshire Quaker who emigrated in 1822, was one of the leading experts on japanning, so the industry got off to a good start. Many of the papier mâché workers were Nonconformists, and a party of them emigrated to Connecticut in 1834 and set up their trade, which became the famous Litchfield Manufacturing Company on the banks of the river Bantam. The most favoured product of the company was its range of richly decorated clock cases, which were sold all over the United States and extensively in South America. The styles of clock had splendid exotic names — The Oriental, the Landscape, The Large Octagon, and the pride of the collection, The Navy Marine, which has decorations in banners, guns, shields, cannon balls, scenery panels, cornucopias pouring out fruit, and the American Eagle standing proudly on the globe, at the top, the whole mass of decoration standing twenty inches high.

Perhaps more familiar to most American readers than their own native papier mâché productions are the Mexican decorative pieces that are mass-produced in a number of studios. The favourite forms are figures, Spanish colonial subjects, coats of arms and furniture covered with little paper squares glued on — sometimes even large pieces of furniture such as pianos. The traditional designs are usually carried out in cord, twisted into decorative shapes and glued to the outside of the papier mâché, after which the whole object is covered with a layer of gesso to make it smooth and ceramic-like.

Papier mâché has had a long and useful existence in the theatre, where its combination of strength and lightness makes it particularly attractive. You will find details in Chapter Seven for making many theatrical properties and aids to scenery, and if you carry out any of these projects you can recall that papier mâché has been used for such purposes ever since the time of Louis XIV (1638–1715), when elaborate scenery and furniture was made up from paper for the court entertainments. Since that time papier mâché has had constant use in the theatre, appearing in all guises from the humble imitations of steaks or pies that constitute most of dramatic catering, to complex pieces of stage furniture and scenery, or the beautiful and dramatic masks made for ballets and Expressionist plays by such designers as Benda and Heinrich Heckroth.

I have said enough, I think, to show that papier mâché is a medium suitable for the most serious artist, while it remains a cheap, easy and accessible medium for the craft worker of even the most modest kind.

CHAPTER 1

General Methods

While the papier mâché works of Henry Clay and others represent a completely durable and tough material, the methods used in early days were often complicated and messy. For many purposes a somewhat less hard-wearing papier mâché is quite suitable, and in any case there are more modern materials than the limited range of adhesives and lacquers available in the eighteenth and nineteenth centuries.

In the chapters that follow you will find instructions for making a great variety of different things, some useful or educational, some decorative, and others for amusement alone. I have tried to make some of the instructions really detailed so that they can be used as a starting point for constructing a number of other models in the same style or by the same method : others of the instructions are less detailed and are intended more as suggestions for the craft worker to develop for him- or herself. However, some of the techniques come up for use in almost every kind of papier mâché work, so this chapter is a general introduction to the essentials of the craft.

Papier mâché can be constructed either by tearing small pieces of paper and sticking them down in layers — laminated work — or by going further and disintegrating the paper into a mass of fibres — pulped paper work.

To do laminated work, you need a fairly hard surface to act as a mould on which to stick the layers of paper. This can be a ready-made surface such as a plastic bowl or plate, or an ornament that you wish to copy, or the plaster cast of some shape. It can also be a shape that you have modelled yourself in

Plasticine or clay, or again a plaster cast made from such a model. It can be a shape roughly made up in wood, wire mesh, cardboard or other materials that you will cover with a layer of laminated paper to strengthen it and build up the modelling. In any case, you tear up pieces of paper into small areas that will fit nicely into the modelling of your mould, dip them in adhesive or brush adhesive over them, and stick them onto the mould. When you have finished a complete layer, go on to make another one, and so on until your laminate is thick enough. You will find details of laminated work in Chapter Two.

Pulped paper is rather like clay, and consists of paper that has been boiled and kneaded until all the fibres are separate. Then the mass of fibres is mixed with adhesive, and usually also clay or plaster to give a smoother product. Pulped paper can be shaped over or in a mould, but it can also be modelled directly, like clay. Chapter Three will tell you more about the pulping process and things that can be made from pulped paper.

PAPERS

The choice of paper for papier mâché depends on the size and strength of the things you want to make. At one end of the scale are tissues of various kinds, that are so soft you can roll them into a kind of rough string when they are wet, and at the other end are the really thick tough papers sold for painting and stencil-cutting, and so on. For laminated work tissues are usually too thin :

you cannot brush paste over them, because they roll up on the brush, and if you dip them in paste they are liable to turn into pulp in your hands. On the other hand, because they are so fine they can often be used for detailed work, in conjunction with other methods. For instance, in Chapter Seven you will find directions for making the actual face part of puppets' heads from tissues dipped in paste and pressed into a mould in the pulpy state that results.

Ordinary cleansing tissues (Kleenex) are quite useful for this sort of work. Do not use paper towels sold for kitchen chores, because they are usually treated by the manufacturers to give them additional strength when wet, and instead of following a shape properly when they are pasted they remain stubbornly in their own original form. Similarly it is very difficult to turn paper towels into papier mâché pulp, because they stand up so well to the boiling and pounding when other papers are easily reduced to pulp.

For middle-weight paper, you need look no further than newspaper. Collect as much as you can — if the papier mâché bug bites you, you will probably start collecting newspapers from other people to keep up the supply. Try to get as many different kinds as possible. You will find when you start on laminated work that it is a great advantage to be able to check when you have finished one layer of paper, before starting the next, and the easiest method of marking this is to use papers that are noticeably different — say ordinary news pages for one layer, and coloured comics for the next, small-ad pages alternating with picture pages, and so on. Most kinds of newspaper are suitable, although you will find when you start to work with them that there are some papers which are softer than others when wet. Save the soft papers for small work where you need to press the paper over sharp details and mould it into little hollows, while the tougher paper will be useful for large models or things that have large, fairly flat surfaces.

Paper from the cheaper magazines is also suitable for larger pieces of construction, but avoid the expensive glossy magazines. The paper in these is very thick and difficult to bend into shape without very obvious creases developing, and often the paper is so thoroughly filled with china clay and similar materials to give a smooth glossy surface that it is difficult to stick layers together, and certainly almost impossible to work such heavy paper into pulp unless you have days to spare for soaking it in water and powerful muscles to pound it into pulp.

If you want unprinted paper, some cheap wrapping papers used in stores may do, but mostly you can work with ordinary newspaper for most of your layers and just add a layer or two of white paper to cover up the print. In any case, printed newspapers and magazines give you something to read while you are working on a model — quite often you see interesting items that you missed the first time round, usually disappearing under a brush full of paste just as you notice them!

If you want really tough paper, particularly for making strong pulped papier mâché, use a long-fibre paper without too much dressing on it. Sometimes you can get hold of the kind of paper that is used for making laminated table tops, and so on, or kraft wrapping paper made for parcel wrapping can be used. If you only need a small quantity, use the kind of heavy drawing paper sold for pastel drawing, but this is rather wasteful considering the vast amount of waste paper that is around, free.

Look around for paper that you can use. Egg cartons (already made of papier mâché pulp) can easily be reconverted into usable pulp for modelling. Clear out your letter files (always a good thing to do — everyone keeps far too much useless correspondence) and use the file copies for laminated paper work. If they have not got much typing on them, the blank pieces are useful for covering laminated work with a final layer of unprinted paper. If your office has a paper shredder, beg a sack of the shreds to make pulped paper (assure the boss, if necessary, that you are not an expert on industrial espionage with a fool-proof machine for sticking the pieces of secret documents together again). Save cardboard-boxes, stiffeners, old file cards — to cut out detailed parts of models like the wings on the dragon in Plate 6. Keep plastic sheet, metal foil, polystyrene foam (Styrofoam) from ceiling tiles and packaging, it will all come in for use.

Papier mâché craft is a truly ecological hobby, recycling waste paper and packaging into useful things again.

ADHESIVES

Next in importance to the paper itself, adhesives are essential for papier mâché, and there are many different kinds with different qualities and uses.

For mixing with the paper in the papier mâché itself, you need an adhesive that will mix with plenty of water. Water is necessary to wet the paper and break down the fibrous structure. The most important of these adhesives are flour paste, starch (wheat) paste, cellulose paste and glue or size.

Flour paste

This is the old faithful adhesive that must have been made in every home at some time. It is easy to prepare, and needs only simple kitchen ingredients and a saucepan. As an adhesive for paper it is in fact rather stronger than starch pastes. It has, however, one great disadvantage. Like the flour it is made from, it is very easily attacked by mould if it gets damp, and as it tends to attract moisture from the air even in fairly dry weather conditions, it gets damp easily. When the mould forms the paste smells musty and unpleasant, and eventually green or black mould or mildew will form on the pasted paper.

In emergency, however, flour paste can be very useful, and the following directions will make up a good paste that is ideal for papier mâché:

Put 3 oz. of flour in a bowl (U.S. readers should use $2\frac{1}{2}$ oz. to allow for the smaller U.S. pint). Plain wheat flour is best, but self-raising flour will do quite well. Mix the flour with a little water at a time, from a measured pint of water, until you have a smooth paste with no lumps. Put the rest of the pint of water in a saucepan and bring it to the boil. When it is boiling, pour it over the flour paste in the bowl, stirring all the time. Now put the thin mixture back in the saucepan and boil for 5 minutes. When cold this will be a thick paste. You can thin it with water if necessary.

This is the basic flour paste. It will keep in the refrigerator without spoiling for 2 to 3 days or a little longer. If you want to keep your papier mâché free from mould, you will need a preservative. See list of suppliers at end of book. For a slight improvement in the keeping qualities of your paste, you can add any one of the following materials (approximate quantities per pint of paste): borax, $\frac{1}{4}$ oz.; oil of cloves, 20 drops; salicylic acid (sold at chemists and druggists for removing corns from the feet — tell them that you want it as a preservative for paste), $\frac{1}{4}$ oz.; formalin (40 per cent solution of formaldehyde B.P. or U.S.P.), 20 drops.

Be careful with all of these materials except perhaps the borax: oil of cloves is poisonous if you drink it, salicylic acid can attack your skin if you handle it in the solid state, and formalin brings some people out in a rash. Better really to buy a proprietary fungicide or use a different adhesive.

Starch paste/wheat paste

This is the usual wallpaper paste made from starch, usually with alum added and often a fungicide to keep away mould. Modern pastes mix very rapidly with cold water and can in fact be added to paper pulp in the dry state to help improve the consistency. For laminated paper work mix the paste as directed for wallpaper, but use less water so that the paste is thicker and stickier.

Cellulose paste

This is the newer kind of wallpaper paste made from methylcellulose, which you sprinkle into cold water and stir. Very soon it makes a kind of stiff jelly that is used for wallpapering. Never use hot water when mixing this type of paste, it will set up into unpleasant sticky lumps that take hours to disperse: always use cold water and add the paste to the water, not *vice-versa*. English readers will be most familiar with this type of adhesive as Polycell: Americans know it as Modocoll. I prefer it for most papier mâché work because it sticks well and is clean to handle. This last is an important point for schools and for parents who want to find a useful activity for their children. Cellulose pastes, the best adhesive for children, do not spoil clothes if they are spilled or dropped — the small shiny patches of adhesive come out at once with washing or sponging with water.

When making papier mâché pulp it is quite convenient to add dry cellulose adhesive to the wet paper pulp and work it in with the hands. It disperses itself in the water contained in the pulp in less than half an hour, leaving a very smooth medium to work with.

Glue and size

These two materials, perhaps the oldest adhesives, are both crude forms of gelatine obtained from bones and other animal waste. They have the advantage that they set hard and tough, but on the other hand they smell rather unpleasant, and they are also subject to attack by mould if the models get damp.

Glue is obtainable in some places in sheets that are melted in water, in others as a powder or crystals. In any case it is necessary to have a double boiler filled with water while heating the glue, otherwise it may burn and produce the most foul smell. Personally, although I know that glue was used by some of the greatest papier mâché craftsmen, I do not like the adhesive for paper work. However, for those who want to experiment, it can be improved in its resistance to water by the addition of linseed oil, as follows:

Swell raw glue crystals by covering them with cold water and leaving them overnight. You should have a thick jelly covered with excess water. Pour off the water from the top and add an equal volume of linseed oil to the jelly. Stir vigorously (you may need to warm the glue slightly to get it to mix easily with the oil). This mixture would be suitable for papier mâché to be used outdoors, although there are other methods of water-proofing that are described later in the book.

Size is just very thin glue solution used to coat paper, to stiffen it and give it a tacky surface. It is not a very useful adhesive compared with modern products.

Dextrin gums

These are the everyday 'office' gums sold in bottles and plastic containers. They are useful for general-purpose paper sticking, and are semi-transparent and clean to use. Dextrin gums are made by boiling starch with acids until it is broken down to a soluble form, dextrin. Many plants contain dextrin as a natural constituent, and in fact the bulbs of some plants contain so much dextrin that they can be used for gumming paper, by wiping the cut surface of a bulb over the paper.

These gums have no particular advantage over cellulose or starch pastes for making papier mâché, but if you happen to have a supply of dextrin gum you can use it just as you would cellulose paste.

OTHER ADHESIVES
PVA Glues

White glue or *PVA glue* is an emulsion of polyvinyl acetate: it is in fact the same sort of material as the base of emulsion paints, without the pigment added. The product is a clear sticky liquid that can be diluted with water to thin it: it is very useful for stiffening paper, and in fact rough shapes for a laminated model can be made up by dipping rolls of paper in PVA glue and letting them stiffen. As it is clean and can be removed with water while still sticky, it is a useful glue for children to use. Marvin medium is one of the PVA glues available in Britain; in the U.S.A. use Wilhold, Sobo or Elmer's white glue.

Clear contact adhesives

These are very useful for sticking parts of papier mâché models together, or for sticking cardboard and other heavier material to a model. Spread both surfaces to be stuck with a little of the glue and let it dry (this drying is important, and you will get a stronger joint if you leave the adhesive to dry thoroughly than if you are impatient), then press the two surfaces together. Try to get the positioning right first time, because it is difficult to separate the pieces again.

These adhesives contain a solvent, so do not use them near flames or while smoking (or too near an electric fire). They are unsuitable for sticking polystyrene foam (Styrofoam) as the solvent dissolves the polystyrene and it shrinks into almost nothing.

British clear contact adhesives are clear Bostik, Evostik, Uhu etc.; in the U.S.A. you can use Duco, Testor's or Elmer's clear contact adhesives.

Epoxy resins

These very hard and tough adhesives are made by mixing one part of the material, in liquid or paste form, with a catalyst that hardens it. Their advantage, apart from their strength, is that there are no solvents to evaporate, so if you fill a space with liquid or pasty epoxy resin, it sets to exactly the same volume of hard solid. For adhesive purposes Araldite is a good British epoxy-resin product. Elmer's or Borden's epoxies are good U.S. I have also recommended in cases that models can be filled with liquid resin, so that it sets up solid inside making a very strong structure. For this you will need liquid resin, as used by garages to mend dents, and by boat-builders. You can buy material from craft shops in the form of transparent resin for encapsulating objects in a hard glassy covering: this is more expensive than the resin used by boat builders and so on, but for small quantities may be more convenient to obtain. Some suppliers are listed at the end of the book.

If you have some of this transparent plastic medium, you can also use it as a strong varnish for papier mâché. This use is covered in Chapter Nine, on finishes.

FILLERS

For making pulped papier mâché and certain other kinds of work, you will need to add other materials to the paper pulp, as well as adhesives. Almost anything that sets to a smooth hard mass will do, and a number of suitable materials are available, mostly in the form of fillers used for stopping up holes in walls.

Plaster of Paris

This is very useful and easy to obtain. Most craft dealers and some builders' supply firms provide plaster of Paris in two grades, normal and extra hard. For filling papier mâché either will do. You can also use the wall plaster employed by builders (Sirapite, Keene's cement; U.S. patching plaster) which sets much slower than plaster of Paris, but as this often contains a quantity of grit or sand it is best used only for large pieces of work where the pulp can be rougher.

When using plaster as a filler, make sure that you mix it well with the pulp and keep it moving: do not let it set into hard lumps. Plaster of Paris gets hot as it sets, and this will give a guide — if you keep the pulp moving until after the plaster has heated up, you will then be sure that it has taken up as much water as it needs. If your pulp sets up too hard for modelling, add a little water and knead it into the mass.

Cellulose fillers

These fillers, such as Polyfilla available only in Britain and Canada can be mixed with paper pulp, and have considerable strengthening action on the finished models. If you mix the cellulose filler with a small amount of plaster you will get a smoother pulp and get over the slight stickiness of the cellulose. With the plaster admixture this stickiness is not apparent, and you can 'stroke' the plaster/filler mixture up to the surface of the modelling to cover up any roughness in the paper pulp.

Clay
Ball clay or ordinary clay for modelling is obtainable from craft shops, and a small amount added to pulp gives a fine smooth surface.

Whiting
This is a form of prepared chalk that used to be sold for making whitewash and similar simple wall paints. It is used extensively in making putty, polishes, and a number of other household products. If you can get hold of good whiting, not too coarse or gritty, it makes a useful addition to pulp, but you may find it difficult to buy these days. Plaster is almost as useful and far easier to find on sale.

CHAPTER 2

Laminated Paper Work

While there are almost countless combinations of different grades of paper, different types of adhesive or binder, and different methods of finishing the work, there are basically only two main types of papier mâché — pulped paper and laminated paper. Although the words 'papier mâché' mean pulped paper, the laminating process is used far more often in practice, and is in many ways more useful, so I shall deal with it first.

Laminated papier mâché consists of layers of paper, previously torn into strips or small pieces, stuck together with paste or glue, usually over a former. Although it is very light, it can be made very strong and tough, especially if the fibres of the layers of paper are arranged in different directions, and properly made laminated paper is often stronger than an equal thickness of wood. By varying the quality of the paper used, and the number of layers, the finished work can be delicate enough for dolls' heads or small toys, or tough enough to make large-scale statuary or even furniture.

PAPIER MÂCHÉ BOWL
The techniques are very simple, but there are a few practical hints that can help produce a good result, and the best way to describe these is to give the details of a simple project, the construction of a laminated papier mâché bowl. These bowls are easy to make and need the minimum of skill, but they can be decorated in a number of ways to make very attractive household gifts that can be used as flower-pot holders for indoor plants,

serving dishes for fruit or nuts, or storage containers. If well made they look almost like china, but have the twin advantages over china that they are very light and almost unbreakable.

Choose an appropriate sized bowl as a mould. Plastic (polythene) bowls are best, as the paper does not stick to the plastic surface, and the flexibility of the bowl makes it easier to detach the finished papier mâché from the mould. If you have to use an earthenware or metal bowl, grease it very thoroughly, as if you were going to cook a cake or pudding in it. (You can, if you wish, grease a plastic bowl as an extra precaution against sticking, but I have never found any difficulty in removing papier mâché from polythene even without greasing).

Now collect a selection of papers. Newspapers are best — try to get several with different appearances, such as small-ads page, comics, pages with several pictures and some with just type, colour pages and so on. This is to help you check on the number of layers you are sticking down. Don't use paper from the expensive glossy magazines with heavy illustrated pages because you will find this too stiff to work easily, and the creases will show in your finished work as lumps or ridges. Similarly, avoid very shiny paper such as glazed notepaper : the surface of papers like these is often made water-repellent, and the paste will not penetrate it properly. Blotting paper and the soft paper sold in art stores for pastel drawing are quite suitable, and build up the thickness of the papier mâché faster, but these papers are a lot more expensive than newspapers.

Mix up your paste. This can be any one of the adhesives recommended on pages 19–21 – if you are using flour paste made at home be sure to remember the warning to add a suitable anti-mould material to the mix, otherwise your papier mâché will begin to smell musty if it gets into a damp atmosphere, and a nicely-made bowl may be ruined by fungus growth. I prefer to use cellulose wallpaper paste, which is clean and easy to mix. Whichever paste you decide to use, make up plenty in a bowl, a little thicker than paste for hanging wallpaper, and find a clean paintbrush about 1 in. across.

Now spread your working surface with plenty of newspaper to protect it, place the plastic bowl on the paper, and begin to laminate. Tear a number of strips of newspaper from one of your stock. Don't cut the paper with scissors, or the sharp edges will show as lines on the papier mâché. The edges of torn paper merge together better. Paste these strips of paper thoroughly, either by dipping them in the bowl of paste or brushing them liberally. The choice is yours, but personally I find the dipping process is messy and there is always a surplus of paste to be brushed off afterwards. In either case, the idea is to soak the paper all through with paste. It is best to paste several strips of paper at a time, letting them have a few moments to absorb the moisture. This makes the paper expand slightly before it is pasted into position, and as it dries it contracts again and wrinkles are pulled out flat.

Cover the bowl with a layer of paper, brushing the strips down smoothly and letting them overlap generously. Don't worry if paper sticks up over the edge of the bowl and on to the paper on the working surface, because you can always cut off any excess afterwards.

When you have one layer pasted on, choose paper of different appearance for the next layer. This makes it easy to see whether you have really covered the surface evenly, or if there are gaps in any layer. Nothing is worse than to complete a complicated piece of laminated work, take it off the mould, and then find that there is a thin place or even a hole because of inadequate numbers of layers in some part. That is why it is so useful to save comics, small-ad pages, coloured papers (like the British *Financial Times*, which is printed on pink paper), and other papers with a distinctive appearance. Carry on pasting layers until you have sufficient thickness – about eight or nine layers are suitable for a bowl – then put the bowl to dry in a warm place.

When the paper is completely dry, it should be quite easy to detach it from the plastic bowl by bending the plastic slightly away from the paper. If necessary, cut away any overhanging paper at the edges that may be obstructing things. You can, if you wish, cut round the edge of the bowl before removing the plastic mould, using the plastic to give you a line, but in this case be careful not to cut the plastic with your craft knife. Trim the edge straight. If you want a really neat rounded edge, paste up some small pieces of newspaper and fold them over the edge (see Figure 1) to make a smooth rim.

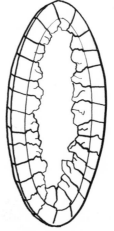

Figure 1. Smoothing the edges of a plate with strips of paper.

When the bowl is dry, rub it over with fine sandpaper to remove ridges and creases still visible, then give it a coat of paint. White vinyl emulsion paint is very suitable, in two

Nineteenth century papier mâché tray by Jennens and Bettridge of Birmingham

Piggy bank in laminated paper.

Ocarina in laminated paper.

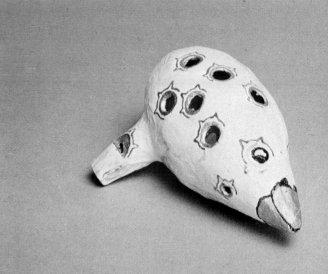

(Left): Hula dancer (laminated paper and pulp over plastic bottle) and llama (laminated paper and nylon cord over plastic bottle). (Above): Owl and Survivalcraft medallion in pulp. (Below): Maraca and dragon in laminated paper.

coats, or you can use gesso prepared as in pages 80–81, or bought ready-made. After painting the bowl should be quite smooth and ready for decoration. This can take any form that you like – floral, geometrical or other designs, or even pictures or silhouettes cut out of magazines and pasted on. More details of finishes will be found in Chapter Nine.

This is the basic laminating process. You can vary it in many ways to suit your own materials and requirements, and the type of work you are doing. For example, you will get a better surface that needs less sandpapering and painting to finish it if you start off with a layer of thin white paper (the thin paper sold for typing carbon copies is ideal, or tissue paper, or even cleansing tissues can be used). This will not be quite an even white, because there will be inevitable differences in the thickness of the paper depending on the amount of overlap you use, but it should cover easily with one coat of paint or gesso.

If you are interested in making designs in *découpage* (see page 79) it is often easier to finish with one or two layers of white or plain coloured paper, and then paste your cut-out pictures or silhouettes, etc., directly onto this. This makes a good school class project, because the children can make a bowl or other simple shape and also get it decorated, all in one period, and the bowls only need a couple of coats of protective clear varnish when they are dry, say the next week, to finish them off.

For large projects, or anything that needs to be particularly strong, use one or two layers of scrim or other openwork fabrics – old net curtains if you have such things are very useful – instead of some of the layers of paper. Dip the scrim in size or thin glue before spreading it over the paper, and let the size or glue set to the tacky stage before adding more layers of paper on top.

Finally, among these general notes on the laminating process, a very small hint if you have a bad memory or have to leave a project in the middle. Nothing is worse than the sudden realisation that you have forgotten how many layers of paper you have applied, and usually it is impossible to tell just by looking at a half-finished laminate. As a check or reminder, you can either put aside one strip of each kind of paper you have used in the layers, joining them with a dab of paste but making sure that each one is clearly visible, as you finish each layer, or you can write the number of the layer in felt-tip pen as you complete it. This is very useful, as I say, if you have to leave the work in the middle.

PLATES, TRAYS AND VASES

Instead of bowls, similar laminated work can be moulded on plates and other utensils. If you are using a china plate, grease it very thoroughly before starting, or alternatively make the first layer of paper *wet* but not pasted. Wet the strips and lay them out to form the first layer, then paste them over to attach the next layer. The wet paper will cling to the plate quite satisfactorily for working, but it will come away easily when the papier mâché is dry. Paper pasted on the base of a large plastic washing-up bowl, and for an inch or two up the sides, will make a useful tray shape for decorating.

When looking around for other household objects to act as moulds for laminated work, make sure that they can be removed from the finished papier mâché skin. Things with waists or necks are obviously unsuitable. The exceptions to this are cases when the 'mould' can be left inside the papier mache as a liner: for example, small jars can be made more interesting by covering them with decorated laminated paper, and the jars left in to form flower vases.

MARACAS

Similarly, the maracas in Plate 6 and Figure 2 were moulded around defunct electric light bulbs with a cardboard tube added as a handle, before the paper was pasted on. When about six layers of paper had been

Figure 2. Maraca from electric light bulb and cardboard tube.

Figure 3. Llama laminated over plastic bottle.

added, the maracas were allowed to dry thoroughly, and then smacked sharply with a piece of wood. The bulb inside broke and the pieces of glass provided the authentic rattle. (It is a tribute to the toughness of papier mâché that I found, making these maracas, that it was quite difficult to smash the glass, even with a heavy blow).

LLAMA

An extension of this work that requires very little skill in modelling is to start with some household object, a plastic bottle for example, and build up from this to some other shape. The llama in Plate 4 was formed very simply from a plastic shampoo bottle with an oval

section (the sort of bottle cunningly designed by the manufacturers to look as large as possible on the store shelf while actually holding very little shampoo). This bottle was cut nearly through in two places, so that it could be bent to form the shoulders and the top of the neck (see Figure 3), and the cap of the bottle formed the llama's muzzle. The bottle was held in the correct shape by stuffing it with roughly pasted paper until the plastic could no longer spring back straight, the muzzle was fixed on with ribbons of pasted paper, and the whole body was covered with one coat of pasted paper to form a suitable surface on which to stick legs and so on. The model was then left to dry.

When it was quite dry, the legs were made from small pieces of cane, wound round with pasted paper, and these were stuck to the body by passing small strips of pasted paper over them. This not only fastened on the legs, but helped to model the shoulders and flanks. The legs were filled out at the top by more paper, the neck and body made to look less starved by the addition of several further layers of paper until smooth curves were obtained, and the ears were cut out of paper and stuck on. The model was then covered completely with layers of white paper and left to dry.

Then, when dry, the llama was sandpapered and painted with emulsion paint in the usual way. The mouth and other details were painted in with poster colour, and the whole model coated with clear polyurethane varnish. The eyes were painted.

The wool was made from a length of decorative cord soaked in polyvinyl acetate emulsion adhesive, and hung in loops from the middle of the back. The first loop, at the shoulders, was pinned to hold it until the adhesive should set, and other loops made successively all round the llama's body. Thinner cord was looped in the same way up the neck, falling just short of the ears and muzzle. The wool was then given flecks of gold from a paint spray, leaving the face and ears white.

OTHER ANIMALS AND FIGURES

Many other animals can be made from plastic bottles in the same way; Figure 4 shows some more ideas that can be worked out in detail by the reader.

Amusing or grotesque human figures can easily be made on the basis of glass or plastic bottles, building up the heads in pasted paper on the neck of the bottle, and details of the bodies on the bulge. These can be quite interesting exercises in 'costume shorthand', creating a type with the minimum of actual details — a yashmak veil and bracelets for the Arab dancing girl, cocked hat and eyepatch for the pirate, and so on. Figure 5 contains some general ideas for such figures. The hula dancer in Plate 4 was made from a washing-up liquid bottle.

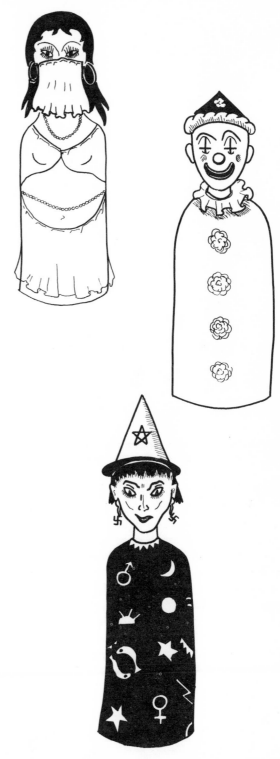

Figure 4. Some bottle animals, showing the plastic bottle former: bull, dolphin, duckling and cat.

Figure 5. Some simple bottle figures: Arabian dancing girl, clown and witch.

27

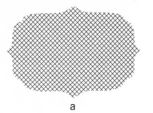 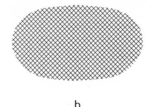 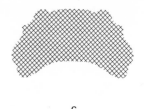

a   b   c

Figure 6. TRADITIONAL TRAY SHAPES
(a) ogee (b) oval (c) 'housemaid's tray' for ease of carrying.

KINDS OF TRAYS

Trays of many different types can be made by pasting layers of paper over a shape cut out of cardboard, thin plastic sheet, or aluminium sheet. Decide on a shape for the tray itself and the handles that are to fasten to it — some of the traditional shapes will be found illustrated in Figure 6. Cut out the handles (see Figure 7), and if the tray is to have sides, fold these up and fasten the corners together with pasted paper or gummed tape and allow this to dry before adding the layers of laminate. Trays of this type were made, usually by pasting paper into a prepared mould, in enormous numbers in the eighteenth and nineteenth centuries, and often decorated by well-known artists, but it is surprising how attractive quite simple designs can be if the tray itself is carefully made. Extra trouble in making sure that the layers are uniform, and careful sandpapering after the tray is dry make sure that the tray is smooth and flat before decoration. If it shows signs of warping during the drying stage, press it down with flat heavy objects onto a flat surface while it is still damp —

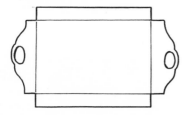

Figure 7. Simplified tray former. Score the cardboard at the sides for ease of folding.

a piece of plywood with weights on it is useful. If you have a flat-topped radiator this is the ideal surface on which to press the tray.

PIGGY BANK

All the objects described up to now have been formed on ready-made moulds, even if they are built up subsequently. Some of the best laminated papier mâché work, however, is done on moulds which are modelled specially. This is not a really difficult operation, even if you are not experienced in modelling, and many attractive and useful objects can be made by this technique. As an example, the piggy bank in Plate 2 was made in less than two hours of actual working time.

The shape is modelled in Plasticine. If you want a small piggy, about 1 lb. of Plasticine is ample: you can save material for a larger model if you use a round bottle as a core and put Plasticine round it. You can make a realistic pig if you like, but piggy banks are traditionally rather shapeless fat creatures, and this simplifies the modelling. Make a sort of large egg-shape in Plasticine, and shape one end for the face and snout. Then fix on the legs and ears.

Paste paper in small pieces over the Plasticine, using the normal precautions to make sure that you have even layers. Smoothing the paper with the hands helps to eliminate wrinkles. Don't try to use pieces of paper that are too large, especially on the very curved parts of the pig, or you will have ridges that won't come out.

It is a good idea to start off the inner layers with one or two layers of plain paper, white or coloured. Smooth paper over the ears and other detailed parts, carefully pushing the paper into recesses such as the space between the trotters. This helps to preserve the details and prevents the animal from being too shapeless. Finish off with a layer or two of white paper. For a substantial pig, I like to use about ten or more layers altogether. Leave the pig to dry in the normal way.

When the pig is quite dry, it has to be split down the middle to release the mould, and then the two halves reunited (see Figure 8). If you have left the outer layer in newspaper it should be fairly easy to see where the join runs from matching bits of print, but if you have finished off in white paper draw a few lines in pencil along the track of the cut, before you start cutting, so that you can see how to join up again.

Remember that papier mâché is tough, especially if it is laminated paper ten layers thick. Use a sharp craft knife with a sawing motion, and be careful that it does not suddenly slip on the hard surface and damage you or the furniture. When the pig is cut in half, carefully ease the papier mâché off the mould. You will probably damage the legs and ears of the mould, and they may even pull off with the papier mâché, but it is an easy matter to model them again if you want to make another copy. Clean up the inside to remove shreds of Plasticine (scrape with a blunt knife), and, if you are really conscientious, paint the inside with a coat of emulsion paint, followed by varnish, because you will not be able to get at it again. When the two halves are dry, hold them together correctly aligned, and paste small pieces of paper over the join. You may have to do this in sections, pasting, say, the middle of the back and letting this dry before you go on to other parts of the join. Sometimes, despite thorough drying on the mould, the halves tend to warp a little: if this happens you will have to bend them into place with gentle hand pressure and hold them aligned until the paper strips dry. Holding the model

Figure 8. Piggy bank. Cut along dotted line to release the Plasticine model.

over a stove is the quickest way and taxes the patience least. Carry on pasting pieces of paper over the split until there is a strong joint. If it seems to be forming an unsightly ridge, spread your paper a little further — if necessary put another layer of white paper over the whole pig, to even things up. Now let the model dry again.

Cut the slot with a sharp knife, and sandpaper the model. You can smooth the edges of the slot with a file or a small piece of sandpaper folded into a thin rod. Paint the pig with gesso or emulsion paint, taking care that the edges of the paper which have been exposed in the slot are well soaked in paint. Now it is ready for decorating.

Decorations for piggy banks are almost unlimited in scope — you can make happy pigs that seem to be glad of their internal prosperity, or sad ones that are obviously begging for more financial food. Unlike real pigs they look well with bright designs on their backs — floral, geometrical, abstract or any other style that you like. Finally the model should have two coats of varnish. Make sure that the slot does not get obstructed during the painting or varnishing.

If you want to make another model from the mould, there are usually two renovations needed. The cut line must be pressed together and smoothed over, and the projecting parts of the design, such as the ears and legs, will almost certainly have to be remodelled.

This does not actually take very long, as the pieces of Plasticine are there and only slightly distorted.

Almost any shape can be fashioned by this technique, as long as it does not have too many undercut parts, and even if it is very complicated you can usually pull the pieces of Plasticine out of the papier mâché a bit at a time. This destroys the original mould, of course, but allows you to model quite freely without thinking about the mechanics of casting, as you must, for instance, with plaster.

OCARINA

The scope for modelling is not restricted to decorations or toys. The ocarina or sweet-potato pipe (Plate 3 and Figure 9) is a working musical instrument that will play as well as a plastic or earthenware commercial instrument, yet can be made in a few hours for virtually no expense except the cost of adhesive, paint and varnish. As a class project, this would be an interesting companion to the maracas described earlier.

The ocarina, to give it its European name, is really an instrument of the recorder or tin whistle family, but made with a bulgy round body instead of a thin straight one. This helps to give it a characteristically sweet and hollow tone, instead of the shrill sound of the tin whistle. Ocarinas were traditionally made in Italy from earthenware, terra cotta, like the Italian carnival whistles from which the instrument was developed in the nineteenth century. Most of them are made from plastic now, if only for the reason that a plastic ocarina is worth picking up if you drop it, while a terra cotta one is not! Laminated paper ocarinas have the same advantage as plastic, because of the strength of the material. The only special precautions that have to be taken are involved in protecting the paper from damp, as will be described.

The shape for the ocarina is very similar to that of the body of the piggy bank, and in fact the main portion of the pig can very well be pressed into service without much modification. The mouthpiece of the instrument should be narrow inside, towards one end (see Figure 10 for scale of dimensions) very narrow near the mouth and widening as it goes into the bulge of the body, and must have thick walls, so start off with quite a thin Plasticine projection and put about two or three layers of paper over it for every one you use on the body of the instrument. To get the best results you need a fairly dense body, so take care to rub down each layer well and avoid air spaces in between. Put on about ten layers of paper and leave the ocarina to dry.

When it is quite dry, cut it away from the mould exactly as for the piggy bank model, and clean out the inside. The next job is to cut the holes for the fingers and thumbs.

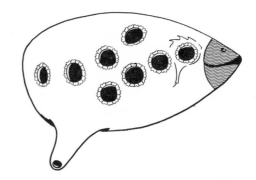

Figure 9. Ocarina (sweet potato pipe). 'Goose' decoration.

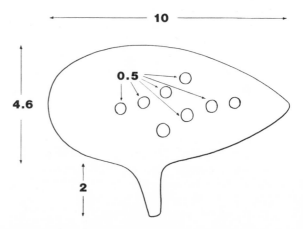

Figure 10. Ocarina dimensions.

30

This can be done when the instrument is put together, but at this stage it is impossible to get at the inside, and you may find that, as you drill the holes, you damage the inner layers of paper. Often the drill will push them away from the other layers as it finally goes through. If you work on the two halves separately you can drill from both sides and get a clean hole much more easily.

Figure 10 gives the layout of the holes, but dimensions will inevitably vary a little with the size and proportions of your ocarina. The layout shown gives notes that are more or less in tune, the dimensions being laid out for a notional ten units. If your ocarina is 10 cm. long, work in centimetres, if 10 in. work in inches, and for other sizes you will have to work out the proportions for yourself. I cannot promise that the result will be perfectly in tune, as the pitch of the notes also depends on the shape and diameter of your ocarina body: if you are interested in making the instruments to play together with others, it would be best to make several ocarina 'blanks', and experiment with the exact layout of the holes.

When the holes are drilled, sandpaper the inside of the two halves carefully and then paint them. As the instrument is bound to get moist when it is played, it is important to make sure that the paper inside is completely waterproofed. I used ordinary household gloss paint, deliberately allowing the paint to soak into the paper. When a coat of paint was dry, I put on another until it was obvious that the paper would absorb no more — the finish changes from matt to eggshell and eventually to a perfect gloss. The edges of the holes needed special care, as all the layers of the laminate are exposed at these points, and paint creeps into the gaps by capillary attraction. Similarly the inside of the mouthpiece, which will be exposed to warm damp breath, needs to be thoroughly soaked in paint.

This technique of waterproofing papier mâché with paint is exactly the same as the old papier mâché furniture makers' method of impregnating their paper with linseed oil and other drying oils, or the oriental workers' use of lacquer, to ensure that the finished work was completely weatherproof. Other materials would do: hard varnish like copal, for example, or epoxy resin (see pages 83—84 for details of the use of epoxy resins as varnishes and waterproofing agents). When halves are quite dry, they should be joined together with strips of pasted paper, exactly as in making the piggy bank, and taking care that the joint is strong. If necessary the whole body can be given one or two more coats of paper to even up the surface, cutting out the finger holes again if they become covered (this will be quite easy, because there will only be one or two layers of paper to pierce).

Now trim the end of the mouthpiece straight and clean, and cut the whistle (see Figure 11 for the shape and position of the hole). It is important that the whistle hole should have sharp, clean edges, so use a good knife blade and try not to make any ragged edges. Now sandpaper the outside of the instrument and paint it in exactly the same way as the inside, taking care to aim for waterproofness rather than economy in paint.

The decoration of an ocarina can be simple or elaborate. The holes, of course, as a fixed part of the design must take pride of place, but you can get quite amusing results if the instrument is decorated as a kind of small fat bird (after all, *ocarina* in Italian means 'little goose').

Figure 11. Ocarina mouthpiece. Note how the walls should be thicker near the outer end.

This book is not an ocarina tutor, but for those who want to play the instrument immediately I have included a simple fingering chart in Figure 12. This will give you the notes of a tune — what the key of the tune will be depends on the size and shape of your ocarina.

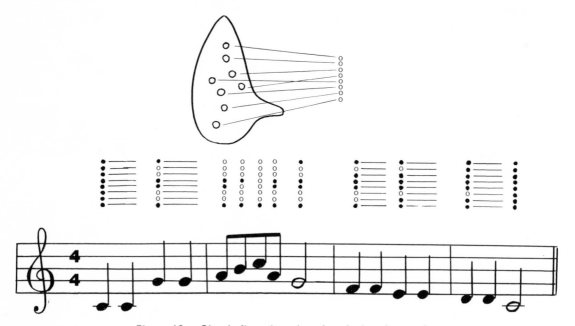

Figure 12.   Simple fingering chart for playing the ocarina.

CHAPTER 3

Pulped Paper Work

If you have carried out any of the projects described in the last chapter, or any other laminated paper work, you will have a fair idea of the advantages and limitations of the laminated method. Laminated paper is very strong, and produces results quite rapidly. On the other hand, the whole business of pasting layers of paper over the mould means that fine detail soon gets blunted and softened, and even if you are careful to rub down and push the paper into hollows, small objects tend to turn into shapeless lumps of laminated paper with no modelling and no character. For some shapes, of course, this does not matter. The piggy bank in Plate 2, for instance, has the same bland plumpness as traditional china piggy banks, and there is not much fine detail to be lost in the laminating process — but for detailed ornaments, doll and puppet heads, small animal models, and other things that ought to have sharp, clear shapes, laminated paper is never really satisfactory. For large work, of course, laminating is quite suitable. The lumps and wrinkles give an interesting 'textured' appearance, and the details are usually so large that the layers of paper do not obscure them.

For any models that need fine detail, and particularly for small work, pulped paper is often far more satisfactory than laminated paper. Properly made pulped paper can be modelled as smoothly and precisely as clay or plaster, and it has advantages over both of these materials, as it is far lighter, tougher, and needs no baking (unlike clay). The pulp takes a little longer to prepare than a laminated paper model, but you can make

up enough pulp for several models at one time, and it keeps for a few days, so a couple of hours' work can keep you in workable pulp for a week.

The essential task in pulp making is to break down the paper to a smooth mass with no lumps. This is not easy, because the paper fibres tend to gather together again even after you have broken them up, but a little patience in the early stages will give you a very satisfactory modelling material.

Take about twelve sheets of newspaper and proceed to tear them into pieces about the size of a postage stamp. This is a long job, is tiring to the hands, and covers your fingers with printing ink, so use the time to meditate or think beautiful thoughts, or even to plan out your next model. Don't skimp this stage : systematic tearing into small pieces will save you a lot of trouble later on. Put the pieces of paper either into a pail of cold water or into a saucepan of water, according to the method you are going to follow.

The paper has to be broken down by the action of water. You can either soak it in cold water in a pail for about twenty-four hours, and then put the pulp in a saucepan and boil it for about fifteen minutes, or you can start off straight away in the saucepan and boil for half an hour. I always go straight for the saucepan, but it must be said that the smell of boiling newspaper is not exactly appetising, and you may prefer to soak first and boil for a shorter time. In any case, it is better to use an old saucepan, as the ink tends to form a scum that is rather difficult to get off.

While boiling, stir the paper constantly with a stick or old wooden fork; this stirring helps to break down the pieces of paper into fibres. By the time you have finished boiling you should have a mass resembling grey porridge, in which none of the actual printing is recognisable. Let this cool.

You can use other papers, of course — unprinted newsprint would be ideal, if you can get hold of it, and some soft writing papers are satisfactory, again if you happen to have a supply. Avoid magazines with the heavy glazed paper used for high-quality illustrations, as the paper does not break down very easily, and do not be fooled by the softness and absorbency of paper kitchen towels and similar domestic wipers into thinking that they will pulp easily. The manufacturers treat these towels to make them resistant to water, and they come out from half an hour's boiling apparently as whole as when they went in. For similar reasons, if you have any left-over *cheap* wallpaper you can pulp it, but most of the better kinds have some plastic coating to make them stronger and more easily washable, and they are almost impossible to pulp satisfactorily.

When the pulp is cold, pour it through a colander or coarse sieve to remove surplus water, and squeeze out some more water by pressing fistfuls between your hands. If you prefer, pour all the pulp into a piece of strong cotton cloth and squeeze out the water by gathering the corners of this and twisting. You should now have pulp that is grey, fairly uniform, and damp but not running with water. If you can see pieces of recognizable print, or feel definite lumps, tear up those bits with your fingers.

Many workers actually rub their pulp against a rough paving stone or some similar surface at this stage to get rid of lumps — Desmond MacNamara, a very fine sculptor who often works in papier mâché pulp, recommends this — but I have found that as long as the boiling and stirring stage is done adequately, there are usually only a few lumps that can easily be torn apart with the fingers and kneaded into a suitable consistency. The more agitation you give the pulp, whether with a stick or your fingers, the sooner all the lumps will be dispersed.

Next you need to add the binding adhesive and materials like clay, plaster, and other fillers to make the pulp smooth and easy to work. The adhesive may be any of the materials discussed in Chapter One — glue, starch paste, cellulose paste, dextrin gum or other adhesives — and the only difficulty which may worry you is deciding how much to put in the pulp. Laminated paper makes this easy, because you make up your adhesive to give the right consistency to paste the layers together, but in pulp work you have to add adhesive to the wet pulp in such quantities that it binds the mass together when the pulp dries.

As a rough guide, I find that the following recipe gives a good pulp, easy to handle and model, which dries to a tough papier mâché. You can vary the quantities of adhesive and filler as your experience dictates.

To every 10 oz. of paper converted to pulp (10 oz. of newspaper is about 50 single sheets of a large-format paper or 100 sheets of a small-format newspaper) add $1\frac{1}{2}$ oz. of cellulose adhesive *or* 4 oz. of cold-water starch paste *or* 2 oz. of glue made up to a thin jelly, and work into this mass 4 oz. of modelling clay *or* a mixture of 2 oz. of plaster (plaster of Paris or ordinary builders' patching plaster) and 2 oz. of cellulose filler. Add water to keep the whole mass moist and rub out the fillers so they are evenly spread through the pulp. This rubbing helps remove the last lumps from the paper pulp making a smooth consistency. Don't add too much water: the pulp will absorb it, but it will shrink all the more as it dries and this could cause you trouble if you are working with moulded models. When you have finished kneading and rubbing you should have a pale mass very much like clay, but rather more elastic.

You can add more clay and/or plaster and filler, and this will make the mass smoother and easier to model. Remember, however, that it will also make the finished models more brittle and heavier — it is the paper fibres that give strength to papier mâché, and the more filler you add the weaker the material becomes. Some of the Victorian home decorations, such as mouldings for ceilings and pelmets, were made with so much plaster that they were virtually plaster mouldings faintly reinforced with paper, and they tend to crack almost as easily as pure plaster mouldings.

The pulp will keep for several days: you can put a damp cloth over it, as with clay, to preserve it from one day to another. If you are using flour paste as adhesive you should add a preservative (see page 19) for any articles that you may want to keep for an extended period.

INSTANT PAPIER MÂCHÉ

If you do not feel like taking the trouble to make paper pulp yourself, you can buy a similar material from craft shops, under the name of instant papier mâché. This is a grey powder made of shredded paper mixed with a suitable adhesive: all you have to do is add water according to the instructions and knead the water in well until the mass is uniformly wet. Do not make it too wet or the pulp will shrink and crack as it dries.

If you make up more of the instant papier mâché than you need, you can keep it for a few days at least by putting it, still damp, in a polythene bag and keeping the bag in the refrigerator. Even with these precautions, however, you cannot expect it to last more than about a week without going hard and losing its plasticity.

Instant papier mâché can be used for any of the purposes suggested for home-made pulped paper. It is, of course, much more expensive than making your own papier mâché.

MODELLING IN PAPIER MÂCHÉ PULP

When you have made your first batch of paper pulp, spare the time to play with it in your hands and get the feel of this new material for modelling. Paper pulp has an elasticity and 'life of its own' which is different from the deadness and subservience of clay or Plasticine, and this may be disconcerting at the beginning. It is not very easy to roll pulp into shapes, as the rolls tend to split in the middle, but it quite easy to pinch and stroke the material to model it. You may find it difficult at first to get sharp lines and ridges, but very soon you will develop the technique of stroking some of the filler up to the surface to give a detailed finish, while the paper fibres underneath give strength and cohesion to the mass. The owl in Plate 5 was made in pulp and deliberately left in a rough state to show the characteristics of the medium: the eyes were simply pushed in and assumed the slightly rounded edges automatically, while the ears were drawn up to their points by stroking the pulp upwards from the head. More working over a model like this would easily give a finish as smooth as clay.

One of the easier pulped paper constructions is a set of buttons or brooches. Japanese *netsukes* will also give you a host of ideas for designs, or you can make heraldic figures, portrait medallions in the Renaissance style, abstract shapes, or any other design that takes your fancy.

First model your design in Plasticine on a small piece of board or the lid of a tin. The size and scale are up to you, but designs smaller than about $\frac{1}{2}$ in. are very difficult to model in sufficient detail to give a proper impact, while buttons or brooches as big as dinner-plates are not very popular! Between one and $2\frac{1}{2}$ in. is a good range of size: the larger ones can be buckles for belts or scarf pins, the smaller ones buttons or ear-clips. Use a small spatula or knife blade, or even a manicure orange stick, to shape your design so that you get clean lines and a neat finish. You can finish the Plasticine surface very smoothly by rubbing it with a little oil and going over it with your finger-tips, gently removing any marks from the spatula or other tools and getting rid of any tiny crumbs of Plasticine that may be loose.

Now build a Plasticine wall round the design about $\frac{1}{4}$ inch higher than the highest point of the relief, and pour in plaster. On this small scale it is important to avoid bubbles in the plaster, and it is often better to paint over the first layer of plaster with a small brush, making sure that it goes into the hollows of the design. Get rid of bubbles by blowing them, and when you have finished pouring the plaster, tap the base board or tin several times to make any recalcitrant bubbles come up to the surface (see Figure 13 for a summary of the casting process).

When the plaster has set hard, pick it out of the Plasticine and clean it with a little dishwashing detergent and water, rubbing it with either a soft brush or your finger-tips to get rid of any loose plaster and the tiny broken-off fragments from the edges that often get into recesses in a casting. Go over it with a spatula or craft knife to sharpen up any points of relief that seem to have lost their definition, and then leave it to dry thoroughly. When it is quite dry, paint the plaster mould with cellulose clear varnish or a solution of shellac. You can buy the shellac from hardware stores — it is the material used for covering knots in wood before painting. Actually any clear varnish would probably do, as long as it is waterproof, as the aim is simply to fill up the pores in the plaster and make it water-resistant. When it is finished, the inside surface of the plaster mould should have a slight eggshell gloss. If it is not glossy at all, the plaster has absorbed all the varnish and it is as well to put on another coat. Finally oil the inside of the mould, using either liquid paraffin or petroleum jelly (Vaseline): you can get Vaseline to spread easily if you warm the mould over a stove or radiator and rub the grease over the inside surface. Make sure that it does not collect in a pool in the lowest part of the mould (the nose of a face mask, for instance) otherwise it will prevent the pulp from filling the space.

Now take a lump of your paper pulp and press it smoothly into the greased mould, taking care that it is pushed well down into the deeper parts of the plaster. Smooth the surface with a spatula or knife blade to give the moulding a flat back, and remove any excess pulp.

The fastening depends on the type of thing you are making. Buttons can have a simple wire eyelet, brooches and scarf pins need a

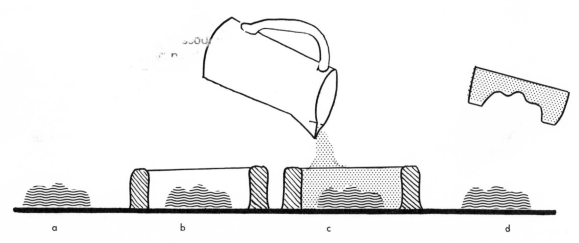

Figure 13. *MAKING A MOULD FOR CASTING PULP BUTTONS.*
(a) Plasticine model (b) wall of Plasticine around model (c) plaster poured in (d) plaster mould removed when wet.

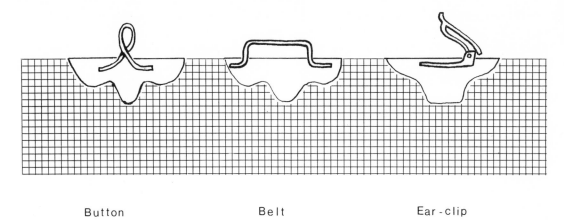

Button   Belt   Ear-clip

Figure 14.   Various fastenings for pulp ornaments.

pin and guard, buckles for belts can be bought complete or made by inserting two wire staples in the back of the moulding. You can get a wide variety of pins, staples, belt buckles and ear-clips for making earrings from craft stores that stock accessories for jewelry making. Wire staples for buttons can easily be made from brass wire, or the wire in safety pins is very suitable. You could also use iron or galvanized wire, but this has to be lacquered after the buttons are finished to prevent it from going rusty (see Figure 14 for fastenings).

Whatever the fixing you use, make small slots in the wet pulp to fit them, smear the slot with liquid glue, and set the fastening in, smoothing over the pulp on top. Put the mould in a warm place to dry, but make sure that it is not too hot, otherwise the pulp will tend to curve backwards as it dries and the work will be warped. When the pulp has dried to a rubbery hardness, remove any shreds of paper which have dried over the edges of the mould with a sharp knife, and ease the pulp out of the plaster mould with a blunt spatula or similar tool. This is rather a tricky operation, but experience will soon teach you the right degree of hardness for the pulp. It needs to be slightly elastic, not bone dry and hard, otherwise it is very difficult to get the pulp out of the mould. Now leave the button, brooch, medallion or

whatever to dry throughout. You can clean up the lines of the design at this stage, working over them with a spatula or knife, and this will improve the sharpness of the relief and also give a slight variation between designs that emphasises the 'hand-made' look.

While one button is drying, you can oil the mould and refill it with pulp for a second one. Of course, if you want a lot of buttons or are in a hurry, you could speed up production by making several plaster casts of the Plasticine original and using them simultaneously. When all the mouldings are quite dry, go over them with fine sandpaper, clean up the edges with a knife, if necessary, and remove any loose fibres from the surface. A good way of doing this is to rub them very lightly with the finest grade of wet-and-dry emery paper and a very small amount of water. Now they are ready for painting.

Any of the methods of painting already mentioned will be satisfactory on pulp. Gesso gives a fine opaque surface, while the effect of pottery can be suggested by painting the pulp with white or coloured vinyl emulsion paint, then picking out the design in poster colour or gouache, and glazing the whole design with clear polyurethane or copal varnish. Attractive results can be obtained by painting over the whole surface with a fairly dark poster colour, then wiping the surface while it is still wet, so that the dark colour remains in the hollows of the design and strengthens the modelling. Ordinary cellulose paint will also work well, and can be applied in the form of an aerosol paint spray if the colour is to be uniform all over. Two coats of cellulose are usually necessary, as the first one tends to soak into the pulp and gives a matt finish. Similarly gold, silver, and other metallic paints can be used, either for base colour or for picking out the highlights of a pattern. Details of all these methods are given in Chapter Nine, pages 80–83.

These small models, buttons, medallions and so on, are very suitable for school class use. Children can design badges for their societies (real or imaginary), for the school or town, or in support of their favourite idol or cause. The modelling in plasticine requires concentration and some neatness, but making the pulp can be made into a pleasantly (but controllably) messy class or group activity. Working in fairly low relief causes no difficulties in the plaster casting stage, and this can be a useful introduction to the whole technique of plaster work.

The Survivalcraft medallion in Plate 5 is a simple example of pulp casting.

Paper pulp is a very useful material for the manufacturer of ornamental mirror frames, picture frames, ceiling medallions and other decorations for the home – indeed, it was used in very large quantities commercially during the eighteenth and nineteenth centuries. Robert Adam, the famous architect and designer, in 1756 commissioned George Jackson to mass-produce papier mâché ceiling medallions, cornices, covings, and other architectural attachments to designs by Robert himself and his brother John Adam. For a period when fashion demanded elaborate decoration of the walls and ceilings of rooms, the advantages were tremendous. Previously all such work was done by very skilled workmen who actually moulded plaster into place on the spot, and with a high and elaborate ceiling this might take weeks. Jackson carved boxwood moulds

which were filled with a mixture of paper pulp, rushes, rag fibres and plaster, compressed the mixture strongly, and dried the pulp. The results were perfect decorations that weighed less than half as much as the plaster ornaments, and could be fixed into position by relatively unskilled workmen in a short time.

It is interesting to note that the original boxwood moulds are still in existence and have been used recently to repair such fine Adam decorations as the Egyptian Hall in the Mansion House, the Clothworkers' Hall and the Drapers' Hall, all in London, and many Adam houses elsewhere. The ready-made pulp decorations became popular in France during the nineteenth century under the name of *carton pierre* (literally, 'cardboard stone').

MOULDING PAPIER MÂCHÉ

While it is very doubtful whether the elaborate fashions in decoration of those days will return, many people still enjoy the richness and craftsmanship of such decoration, whether it be Adam, with their classical restraint, or the more opulent styles of rococo or Louis Philippe. It is fairly easy for the papier mâché worker to satisfy this requirement, and the results can look just as convincing as original plaster or wooden ornament.

As an example of this work, Figure 15 shows some of the stages in the production of a frame for a mirror, in the style of Robert Adam. The mirror itself was a rather cheap convex mirror on a plywood backing with no frame at all: the design was not a direct copy of any of Adam's mirrors, but was sketched out from some of his favourite *motifs*.

The frame was moulded in Plasticine on a piece of board. To help with the symmetry and precision of the modelling, I drew out half of the pattern in detail on drawing paper, then folded the paper and traced the other half. I made *two* copies of this, one for reference and the other to tack to the base board. This pattern helped to make sure that the Plasti-

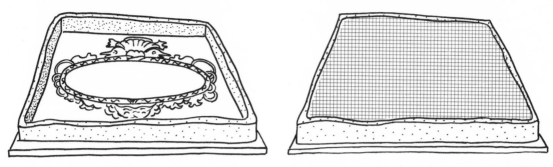

Figure 15.   Pulp mirror frame. The model is surrounded with a Plasticine wall and plaster poured in.

cine model was properly shaped and symmetrical, at least in plan.

When the modelling was complete I built a Plasticine wall round the model, just as with buttons and medallions, and mixed up some plaster. The whole mould took about 7 lb. of plaster, but it is better to mix up about 1 lb. at a time at the beginning of the casting.

When casting a large piece of work like this the plaster must be reinforced with scrim, pieces of sacking, old bandages or any other open type of material. Sometimes vegetables come in openwork sacks — these are very useful for reinforcement. Have ready a supply of strips of such material before you start casting.

Splash the whole surface of the plasticine model with plaster mixed to the consistency of thick cream, making sure that the whole surface is covered and that air bubbles have been brushed out (use a soft brush or your fingers). Carry on pouring of the first layer plaster until it is all in the mould. Then mix up a new batch of plaster, coat the first batch with wet plaster, and dip the scrim, bandage or other reinforcement in plaster and lay it over the mould, with plenty of crossing and overlap to add to the strength of the structure. Then pour on the rest of the plaster. Go on like this until the mould is about $1\frac{1}{2}$ in. thick, or at least $\frac{1}{2}$ in. thicker than the most raised part of your model. Then leave the plaster to dry and harden.

To get the Plasticine master copy out, it is best to hold the plaster under a tap and prise out the Plasticine with a blunt knife or spatula. Clean out the mould with dishwashing detergent and water, and leave it to dry thoroughly in a warm place. If you should be unlucky enough to crack it, the scrim will hold it together, and you can repair it by damping the plaster and applying a fresh coat of plaster on the back to hold the parts rigid.

When the plaster is quite dry, seal it with cellulose varnish or shellac, and oil it with liquid paraffin or petroleum jelly, as described on page 36. It can then be filled with pulp.

As paper pulp contracts rather a lot as it dries, large pieces of work such as this are best made by a combination of pulp and laminated paper. The pulp is used for the fine detail, laminated paper to provide a strong skeleton for the structure. Press a layer of pulp into the plaster mould so that it fills all the troughs and hollows, and cover the inside of the mould with a layer of pulp about $\frac{1}{4}$ in. thick, no more. Leave this to dry until the surface of the pulp is beginning to toughen up, but it is still obviously damp, then cover it with cellulose paste or glue, whichever you use for laminated paper, and put on layers of laminated paper, using pulp to fill in details at the edges. Press down all the layers as you put them in, so as to make sure that the pulp is still filling every hollow. Finally fill up the mould level with pulp and leave it to dry to the tough rubbery stage at which it can be removed. Work over the decoration to sharpen up details, then leave the papier mâché frame to dry thoroughly.

When the frame is quite dry, go over it with sandpaper or wet-and-dry emery paper to smooth it off, and gild it or paint it as you wish. If it is a mirror frame you can staple it to the wooden back of the original mirror, or use small brass plates to fix it, or even mount the whole assembly, mirror and frame, on a sheet of plywood cut to suitable shape with a fretsaw. Staples or brass plates are better for the more florid type of frame, as the plywood backing tends to detract from the lightness and delicacy of the frame.

Similar work can be done with picture frames, using a fairly thin pulp moulding stuck onto a simple wooden picture frame with glue, and if you are ambitious you could try such articles, beloved of the Victorians, as bedheads and clock-cases.

The combination of pulp and laminated paper can be a very useful one if you are making such models as portrait busts, animals, and other objects requiring a fair amount of detail. The shrinkage of pulp makes it unsuitable for really large work, but if things are made in laminated paper, the fine detail can be over-modelled on the surface in paper pulp, thus combining the advantages of both methods of working. Some of the more elaborate projects described later in this book depend on this combination of methods.

CHAPTER 4

Some Other Techniques

The last two chapters will have given you an idea of the scope of laminated and pulped papier mâché applied in or over various kinds of mould. There are, however, a number of papier mâché projects that can be carried out without making a conventional mould, and the following methods are described mainly as starting-off points for you to invent new techniques of your own.

APPLIED DECORATION

Many pleasant objects can be made by a synthesis of paper sculpture and laminated papier mâché. For example, if you have a large plain can or bowl, you can change it into a classical-style garden urn by adding fleurs-de-lis or acanthus decorations. Figure 16 shows the stages of work.

First cover the can or bowl with two or three layers of plain paper or newspaper so that you have a smooth paper surface to work on. Now cut out the shapes of your decoration in fairly thick paper — drawing paper is excellent for the purpose — producing as many leaves, etc., as you need for about eight layers of paper (the number of layers

will depend mainly on the thickness of the paper you use). You can duplicate the leaves either by tracing from one master copy, or by a pricked stencil. Take a sheet of cellulose acetate film rather larger than your leaf or other decoration, pin it down over the drawing, and prick round the outline with a very small awl or a needle stuck into the end of an old penholder.

Where the needle has gone through the plastic, there will be a small projection of little spikes sticking up on the back. If you place the plastic sheet on your drawing paper, with a sheet of pencil carbon paper (not typewriting carbon) in between, and rub gently over the pattern, you will find that you can transfer the pattern in the form of a line of little dots. It is quite easy to cut along the lines made in this way. Alternatively you can use the same acetate stencil, and mark through it with black poster colour or some similar dark paint, dabbed through the holes with a stencil brush.

Dip each leaf in turn in white glue, and smooth it into position. If you want the leaves to curl outwards at the top, make this curl

Figure 16.   Coating a can with cut-out laminated ornaments.

after you have stuck on about two layers, and let the leaves dry until they are stiff.

When all the leaves have been built up, paint the whole object with household gloss paint. This will soak into the paper, and you will need to put on two or three coats to get a good finish, but the intention is to impregnate the paper with paint to make it as waterproof as possible. If you want a slightly matt finish, like stone, use eggshell gloss for the last coat of paint, or go over the gloss paint with very fine wet-and-dry sandpaper when it is dry.

The same technique, cutting out shapes in paper and then building up layers of these pieces into a relief, can be used for all sorts of shapes and patterns. Often an interesting effect is achieved if the relief is rounded to some extent by cutting the upper layers successively smaller than the lower ones. For example, if you want to make a pattern of vine leaves and grapes, cut the shapes for the leaves all the same size, so that the edges of the leaves stand out sharply, but make the grapes of circles with steadily reducing diameter, so that they are rounded in section as well as in plan (see Figure 17). Very often people who would say that they 'cannot model anything' find that this technique, which is based far more on drawing than modelling, comes very easily. The results look rather like paper sculpture, but are far stronger and permanent.

One particular application of the technique is the manufacture of coats of arms in relief. Modelling in papier mâché pulp or instant papier mâché, however skilfully done, is hardly precise enough to give the sharp geometrical lines required for heraldic work, but working with layers of paper cut to shape gives a very crisp effect.

PAPIER MÂCHÉ OVER FOLDED PAPER

It is not necessary to make a Plasticine or similar mould for laminated papier mâché if you have some other centre rigid enough to hold some layers of paper. For example, simple but attractive Christmas tree decorations may be made from origami paper boxes with a few layers of extra paper pasted over them. Such boxes are much stronger than the original folded paper and will keep from one Christmas to another.

To make the boxes that form the centres, start with a square sheet of paper. Brown wrapping paper is quite good, but typing paper can be used. A sheet 8 in. square makes a box which is about 2 in. along each side, so you can work out the size you need according to the scale of the boxes you decide to make.

Figure 18 gives the essential folds for origami boxes. The first folds are along each diagonal of the square sheet, folding forwards, and straight across parallel with the sides, folding back. Fold in along this line so that the paper has four triangular 'wings' (Figure 18a). In each of these triangles in turn, fold up A to meet B (18b) then fold in the tip of C of these new triangles to the middle (18c). Fold down and outwards from B to make a flap D, and crease this flap across the middle (18d). You will then find that the creased flap D can be slipped into the gap next to it (18e) in each of the four 'wings' of the paper. When all four flaps have been slipped in so that they are held tightly, inflate the box by blowing through the hole at the end.

When you have made your boxes, ease them into the right shape with your fingers (you can make them almost perfect cubes by folding the remaining edges, or they can be blown out until they are almost spherical) and paste small pieces of paper over the

Figure 17.   Laminated decorations — square and rounded edges.

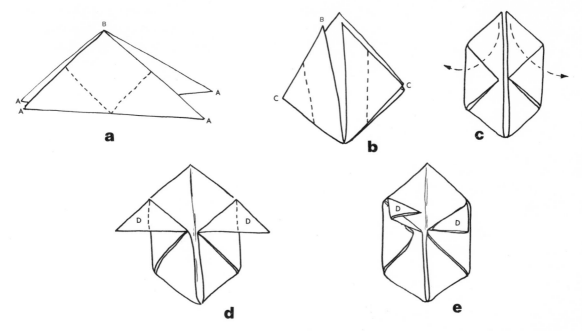

Figure 18.   Stages in folding a paper box.

box, covering up the flaps and fold. Don't put too much paper on at a time or your box may get soggy: if you are making several decorations it is best to put one layer of paper on one, place it on a radiator or other warm place, and carry on with another while the first one dries a little. When you have enough layers of paper, leave the boxes to dry and paint them as you wish: fluorescent poster colours look rather well on them. Make a hole at one corner and fasten string or wire to hang the boxes.

Dragon and other monsters

Another model made without a mould is shown in Plate 6 and Figure 19. The dragon's body was made over a cardboard cylinder from a toilet roll, and the tail, which can be moved about, was made by constructing a number of circles of gummed tape of various sizes. The tape was wetted and rolled into cylinders, then left to dry so that the cylinders were quite hard and rigid. Each one was cut at one end to resemble scales, and the cylinders were then fitted

into one another to make a gradually diminishing tail. The last one was fitted with the tail fin. These could be stuck together, of course, but a better effect is obtained by making small holes in the top and bottom of each cylinder (Figure 20) and fastening them together with paper fasteners. The knobs of the paper fasteners on top can be disguised by putting projecting fins over them, or they can be worked into

Figure 19.   Dragon.

43

Figure 20. Dragon's tail in sections fitted together with paper fasteners.

the general decorative scheme. If you use only one paper fastener per cylinder, the tail is weaker but more flexible. You can decide how many to use according to the amount of handling you expect the model to undergo.

The legs were made of laminated paper rolled over wire and stuck to the rest of the body with layers of pasted paper. The fin on the back was made of packaging foil fastened into a slot cut in the back, and the head was modelled over wire. The wings were cut out of thin card and built up rather like the applied laminate models, using steadily diminishing pieces of card (Figure 21). Painting a dragon is an opportunity for sheer fantasy, so I do not propose to lay down any instructions for this.

If you are interested in the natural history of such monsters, you can build up a whole menagerie of mythical beasts. The *wyvern*, for instance, is a dragon depicted in heraldry and usually has a twisted tail, sometimes tied in a knot. If you decide to make one, use a lot of small cylinders in the tail to give flexibility. The *griffon* has an eagle's head, shoulders like a lion, with lion's feet and claws, and a dragon's tail. The *cockatrice* has a cock's head and wings, and a dragon's tail, the *chimera* has a lion's head, a goat's body and legs, and a dragon's tail, while the *echidna* and the *basilisk* are really serpents with human heads, the echidna having a woman's head and the basilisk a bishop's head in a mitre.

Figure 21. Dragon's wing laminated from paper cut-outs.

CHAPTER 5

Educational Projects

Apart from its obvious advantages as a craft for carrying on in schools, papier mâché has many uses in the understanding of other subjects. Many concepts that are difficult to put over and difficult to understand from two-dimensional diagrams and pictures can readily be understood from a three-dimensional model, and papier mâché has all the merits of lightness, cheapness, and the ability to take any shape, required by a good three-dimensional modelling medium. Here are a few suggestions for its use.

RELIEF MAPS

Relief maps are the best way to understand the real geography of an area, or to explain such earth structures as faults and anticlines. River catchment areas, so hard to distinguish from an ordinary map, become immediately obvious when the various slopes and valleys are seen in 3-D. On the other hand, relief maps have to be fairly large, and if they are made of plaster they are both heavy and fragile, apart from the fact that the plaster is very awkward to model. The following method for making laminated paper relief maps gives a strong, light model that is ideal as a subject for group activity in geography classes.

First, obtain a base board. This need not be very strong as long as it is thick enough not to bend too much — plywood or chipboard would be ideal. Cover this with thin white glue or animal glue and spread thick white paper (drawing paper) or thin white card all over it. This gives a good surface for drawing, and also makes a suitable surface on which to stick the supports for the relief map. As the glue dries, start transferring the contour lines from the map of the area to the base board. It will be obvious that the best way to do this is to square off, as artists do when scaling up a picture from a small study to a large canvas or wall. Divide the map area into a number of equal squares, and draw the same number of squares on the base board (if you do not want to mark the map, draw the small squares in Indian ink on a piece of acetate sheet, and lay this over the map so that the contour lines show through). Use the squares as a guide to transfer the contour lines onto the base board, using a felt tip pen or similar instrument. Mark each contour line with the figure for its height.

When the contours are marked, decide on a height figure that represents the lowest point of the area, and the highest point, and decide on a scale of heights for the model. If, for example, your map goes from 1,000 ft. to 2,000 ft. in 50-ft. contours, you may decide to construct the model with a scale of 1 centimetre height for every 50 ft. which will make a very exaggerated map unless you have a large base board, or you may find that $\frac{1}{2}$ cm. to 50 ft. is more realistic. In general it is best to exaggerate the heights, in proportion to the horizontal distances, quite a lot, otherwise even the Rockies come out like slight folds in the surface of the map. This is a problem that the class can discuss with some profit.

Suppose you have decided on $\frac{1}{2}$ cm. to 50 ft. and the heights range from sea level to 350 ft. The base board represents ground at sea level. Cut a long strip of cardboard

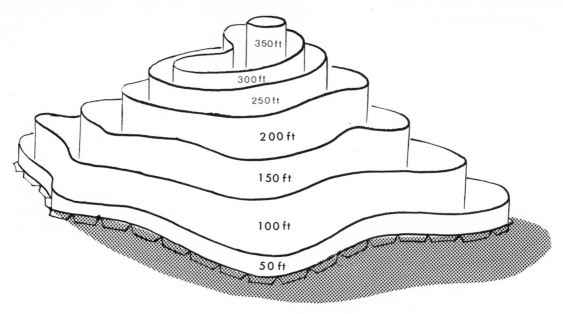

Figure 22.   Relief map — contours ready for covering.

(fairly thin card, but thick enough not to flop about) $1\frac{1}{2}$ cm. wide. Fold it so that it has one piece $\frac{1}{2}$ cm. wide to form the 50 ft. contour line, and a 1 cm. piece to stick to the base board. Cut little V-shaped pieces out of the 1 cm. side to allow the card to be curved along the contour line (see Figure 22). Now coat the 1 cm. strip with white glue and stick it down to the base board so that the $\frac{1}{2}$ cm. portion sticks up like a little wall. The contour can be followed with several pieces of card if the first one is not long enough. Now cut card 2 cm. wide, and bend it so that there is a 1 cm. 'wall' to represent the contour at 100 ft., and again a 1 cm. strip to stick down to the base board. Go on like this until every contour line is represented by a little wall of the right height: the result will look like an odd-shaped maze or a crazy defence system.

Now take small pieces of thin card, similar to the material you used for the contour lines, and stick these with white glue to the tops of the contour 'walls', so that the whole structure is smoothly roofed in. Card is better than paper for this purpose, because wet paper tends to sag into the gaps

between the contour 'walls' and makes a series of furrows instead of a smooth sweep of surface. When the card is dry (use small pieces so that there is no danger of introducing creases that have no geographical origin) cover the whole assembly with three or four layers of pasted paper, followed by two coats of white paper. This should now follow the contours of the area exactly. When the paper is dry, paint it with emulsion paint or gesso, and paint in any details such as rivers, etc., that you wish to demonstrate (snow line, tundra, towns and villages and so on). Then for protection it is better to give the whole surface a coating of clear polyurethane varnish to waterproof it. (Of course, if you intend to mark in geographical details during a class, leave the varnish off until this is done. The emulsion paint will take poster colours very well, but only oil or acrylic paints can be used after the varnish is applied).

This technique can be applied to almost any contour system, from the smallest hill-fort to the largest geanticline. All you have to do is to decide on your scale. The great advantage that the laminated paper surface has over plaster or similar solid modelling media is that even if the top surface becomes detached from the cardboard contour lines, it will not lose its shape, and it could easily be remounted on any base board.

BIOLOGICAL MODELS

As papier mâché is so easy to shape into curved and involuted forms, it is ideal for making three-dimensional biological models for demonstration. Figure 23 shows the stages in making a model of a human hair in its follicle, with all the surrounding skin organs.

The 'skin' portion of the model is a layer of papier mâché pulp about 2 in. thick, spread on a wooden base board. The top surface can be levelled with a rolling pin or similar instrument. Put the pulp to dry, and roll it to make sure that it remains flat.

When the pulp is drying but by no means completely hard, sketch the lines of the follicle and the position of the surrounding features such as the sebaceous gland, the *arrector pili* muscle and the blood stream to the hair root. Gouge out the damp pulp from the hollow part of the follicle and press it into a neat half-cylindrical shape by means of a piece of round wood or similar round tool. Now leave it to dry thoroughly.

To make the 'hair' itself laminate paper round a suitable tube, glass or plastic. Part of the hair is cut away at the top to show such features as the medulla and the spindle-shaped cells of the cortex, and you may care to make some of the cuticle scales detachable to show their imbricated nature. When the model is completely made up, it can be covered with emulsion paint and the details painted in with poster colour. With a final coat of polyurethane varnish the demonstration model is complete.

The combination of pulp for large surrounding areas and laminated paper for details will be found suitable for many other biological structure models.

MATHEMATICAL MODELS

Three-dimensional models for demonstrating solid geometry and similar subjects can often be made of paper or cardboard, but if they have curved surfaces this becomes more difficult. Laminated paper over a curved mould can be made to take almost any shape – solids of revolution, three-dimensional graphs with curved surfaces, models like the double cone cut to show the formation of the parabola, hyperbola and ellipse, can all usefully be made in laminated papier mâché.

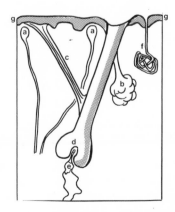 

Figure 23.   HAIR   MODEL
(a) nerve cells   (b) sebaceous gland   (c) arrector pili *muscle   (d) papilla   (e) blood vessels   (f) sweat gland   (g) epidermis   (h) hair root   (i) cuticle   (j) cortex   (k) medulla.*

CHAPTER 6

Large Constructions

STATUES

Papier mâché, apart from its other advantages, has ideal qualities for really large pieces of work. The cost of clay or stone for a full-size statue, for instance, is well beyond the means of most amateur artists, but such a statue can easily be made in papier mâché for no more expense than a few bundles of old newspapers and some paste or glue. In addition, the papier mâché model can be carried around and placed anywhere for display — with stone or clay one has to think carefully about the strength of floors and supports.

Large projects in papier mâché can be carried out in sections, which makes it very suitable for school class use: children can have the pleasure of creating large and impressive figures or other constructions in group work, whereas this would not be possible with other modelling media, apart from the cost.

Classical statuary effects can be obtained by making a wire armature, covering it with wire mesh in places, and coating this in scrim dipped in plaster. This shape is then covered with pasted paper. The technique is described more fully in Chapter Seven in connection with stage statuary as items of scenery.

Another type of construction that is very suitable for school or club use is the building-up of lifelike figures in contemporary clothes. Such figures can be used for drawing attention to club activities such as dances and barbecues, for advertising charity and church collections and appeals, or for any other purpose where an eye-catching three-dimensional display will get publicity. Papier mâché is the ideal medium for window-displays in stores, and many clever pieces of advertising have been created in this way.

Emergency Scene

Suppose, for example, you want to publicise a charity appeal for the Red Cross. Good posters and striking wording will get you a lot of attention, but a life-size emergency scene, with nurses, a doctor, and injured people will have far more impact. There is no reason why such a display cannot be made in quite a short time by a few pairs of willing hands, and the finished models will be light enough to be carried around in the back seats of cars or in a small pick-up truck.

Take the figure of a nurse first. If the figure is to be free-standing, you will have to find two pieces of wood about 5 ft. 3 in. long to act as the armatures for the legs, and to go right through the model as supports (see Figure 24). These are fixed together at the top and placed in the right position for the legs. If the model has a base-board, which is the most convenient construction, fix the legs to it with strong brackets: these can be disguised as the feet later on. Across the shoulders fix a suitable length of stiff wire to form an armature for the shoulders and arms. It can be fastened to the wooden supports with staples. Two thicknesses of medium wire twisted together are even more effective than one thickness of thicker wire, as the twists give more grip to the papier mâché which goes over the wire.

Make up the shape of the skirt in wire mesh, and similarly the top of the body, and

48

(Right): Breakable Buddha for stage work. (Below): Furniture for puppets' or dolls' houses.

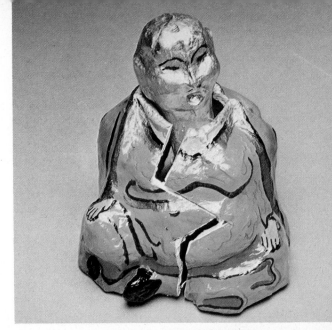

Thai dancer's mask and Thai doll with papier mâché mask.

Congolese mask and Thai clown's mask.

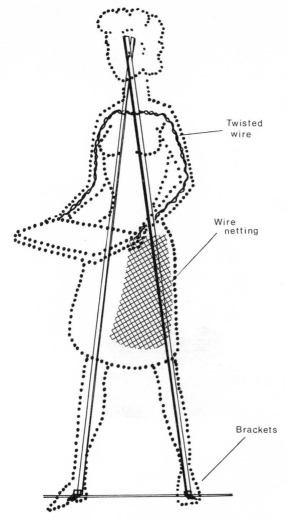

Figure 24. *Supporting a life-size figure. The skirt in this figure is shaped from wire netting.*

Labels in figure: Twisted wire, Wire netting, Brackets

solid as the paste dries, and will give you quite a firm surface on which to model. Lastly model the feet with small rolls of paper.

You can now go over the whole model and make the surfaces smoother by pasting paper strips and modelling the finer detail. Don't try to be too precise or you may lose some of the impact of your display. Lastly cover the model with white paper and leave it to dry. Then paint it with emulsion paint and leave it to dry, paint in the features and details of the clothes with poster paint, and give it a coat or two of clear polyurethane varnish. Properly done, this will keep your display weatherproof, even outdoors, for a few days at least.

Variations on this simple model are legion. You can, for instance, have more lifelike clothes by sticking the appropriate cloth on the outer layers, or even dressing the model in real clothes (in the case of the nurse, for instance, a genuine nurse's uniform). Hair can be made in any degree of naturalism from painted hair or unravelled jute or string (or even wood shavings), through hair made from theatrical crêpe hair, to the use of an actual wig.

Bodies and other bulky items can be made by stuffing newspapers into an old sack and then tying it to make the waist, or by making rolls of paper tied up (see Figure 25) and sticking these together into the right shape.

cover the mesh with a layer of pasted paper to act as a foundation for further work. Model the arms and the lower part of the legs below the skirt by making small rolls of pasted paper. If your nurse is to wear slacks and not a skirt, you can model all of the legs in this way and just use wire mesh for the hips.

The head is started by stuffing lightly pasted paper into an old stocking or leg of a pair of tights cut off, and then built up with pasted paper strips to model the features. If you put the stuffed stocking to dry in a warm place, you will find that the paper inside sets up

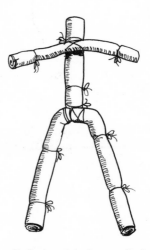

Figure 25. *Rolled and tied paper for large figures.*

Models like this are of course somewhat heavier than the completely hollow kind made on a wire and mesh armature, and take longer to dry because of the weight of damp paper they contain.

For more complicated models you can make a complete armature in wood or heavy wire expressing the pose, and then cover this with pasted rolls of paper. This method is better if you have fingers bending or stretching, or if the knees are bent, as you then have a firm support for the wet paper. When it is dry, the paper will account for most of the strength of the model, but while it is wet it cannot be expected to hold a difficult pose.

For school group activities, it is probably best if the group produce a sketch, however rough, of their model before they start, so that everyone is clear on the pose and the basic proportions. Measuring up arms, legs, length of body, and so on will teach children quite a lot about elementary anatomy and will tend to make them better at figure drawing, whether the model they are making is a cave man or the latest pop star. There is something very satisfying about making a full-size human being — the class groups will begin to understand the feelings of Pygmalion or even Dr Frankenstein!

LARGE TOYS

Papier mâché toys have many advantages: they are cheap and light, they are more or less non-poisonous as long as you keep to the commoner adhesives, and they are safe for children if you avoid such things as sharp wire armatures near the surface. If they are home-made, from almost free material like old newspapers, no one is going to be very sorry when at last they disintegrate.

Rocking Horse

Some toys, particularly trains and trucks and similar things with straight lines, are probably better made in wood or hardboard (Masonite), but if the shapes are curved and complicated then papier mâché scores every time.

The simple rocking horse illustrated in Figure 26 is an example of a large toy made from the simplest household materials and entails only a very small amount of carpentry.

The rocking portion of the toy, for strength

Figure 26.   Rocking horse.

and ease of construction, is made of wood as a kind of rocking stool. The rockers and their legs are fastened to a flat piece of wood which forms the base on which the horse's body is built up. The rockers can be made, preferably from some hardwood, with very simple carpentry tools, or you might even be able to find the base of a broken rocking chair or similar piece of furniture to save some of the work. The legs are best made from ready-shaped coffee table legs with screw plates at the top. Remove the metal feet from the commercial legs and cut dowel holes in the rockers to take the ends of the legs: these are fixed in with glue or epoxy adhesive. The ends of the legs with screw bolts are fitted to the flat wooden base exactly as if you were fitting legs to a coffee table. Add a little epoxy adhesive dabbed on the screw threads when screwing in the legs: this makes them stand up better to the vibration of rocking.

Now build up the body on this base. The idea is to make as much of the shape

50

from ready-made objects as possible, before you start to put on the layers of paper. So the horse's ribs are shaped on a one-gallon plastic bottle, as sold with liquid detergents and similar materials in bulk. The head and neck are cut out from hardboard (Masonite) to get the right shape, and then swelled out with rolls of pasted paper pressed onto the sides. The hardboard is fitted to the wooden base of the horse with a small metal bracket. All this sounds terribly rough and unworkmanlike, but of course these fixings are only intended to hold the parts together until the papier mâché is dry. Once the horse is covered with laminated paper and this has hardened, the papier mâché will contribute all the strength needed, and all the rough and makeshift fastenings will be covered by a strong layer of laminate.

Now prepare armatures for the legs. These are best made of twisted wire, which holds the wet papier mâché better. Build up the shape of the legs to some extent before fitting the legs, by winding pasted paper round the wire. Then fix the legs to the body with strips of pasted paper, and build up the shoulders and flanks over the top of these joins — the layers of paper will help the modelling and at the same time fix the legs more securely. A nail through the legs to the wooden base (Figure 27) helps to keep them secure. Now cover the whole horse with layers of pasted paper: the more the better, as this will make a strong and long-lasting toy.

When you have built up the shape completely, cover it with a layer of white paper and leave it to dry. This will take some days because of the weight of damp paper in the construction, but be patient. Then sandpaper and paint. I prefer to use household gloss paint for such models, deliberately letting it sink into the paper. You may need three coats to get a glossy finish, but all the paint will help to waterproof and strengthen the papier mâché. If there are any gaps where you can get at the inside of the model, turn it upside down and pour a little paint in to soak into the inner layers of paper. Now decorate it in acrylic or oil colours. Rocking horses, I

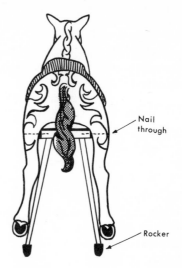

Figure 27.   Fixing the rocking horse to its stand.

Figure 28.   A chain through the mouth makes a bit for the rocking horse.

think, ought to have the same flamboyant colours as the old-fashioned roundabout (carousel) horse, but if you know that the recipient has a yen for a chestnut, white, piebald, skewbald or even pink horse the decision is made for you.

The mane and tail can either be made as part of the papier mâché shape, or they can be stuck on with horsehair or raffia afterwards. The papier mâché kind look more artificial but tend to last longer.

Reins can be fixed to a bit made by boring

a hole through the mouth portion of the head and fixing a small length of chain through this. Fasten a ring on each end of the chain (Figure 28) and fix your reins to these. Last of all, varnish the papier mâché and wooden portions of the toy with polyurethane varnish.

A Modern Children's House
You can use papier mâché for many other large toys, and it has particular utility when curved surfaces are needed. There are many attractive toys that can be made out of wooden and cardboard boxes, but the straight lines and right angles make the models look very boxy indeed. Papier mâché surfaces in suitable curves will make a simple toy look much more professional. If you are making a spacecraft or plane, for example, a curved control board or even a shaped seat will cover up very simple construction. Similarly you can create the most modern styling for the ordinary soap-box buggy in papier mâché over wire netting.

Instead of the usual kind of children's garden house, why not make a really modern construction based on a dodecahedron? Get plenty of garden wire, stiff enough to hold itself straight but not too difficult to bend with pliers, and make twelve pentagons with sides about 18 in. long. Use lengths of wire that are five-and-a-bit times the length of the side: for example, if you stick to 18 in. sides cut your wire to about 96 in. Fold the wire at the angles with pliers, and finish off the extra length to lie alongside the first side (see Figure 29). When you have made these wire pentagons, cover the wire with strips of pasted paper. This will also hold the two ends together. Leave two of the pentagons unfinished, i.e. with one side of each uncovered. These pieces of wire will eventually be cut away to make the door, but it is easier to make all the shapes the same in the first stages.

Now you must connect all the pentagons together to make an openwork solid figure. Take three of them and fasten the adjacent sides together with thin wire, pipe cleaners or adhesive tape, and coat with strips of pasted paper wound round (Figure 30) so that they have a shape like a very shallow basket. Make up the other pentagons into threes in this way, making sure that the bare wire sides of the two unfinished ones are placed next to one another — these bare wire sides need not be covered with paper unless you want to put one or two strips round to hold the shape during construction. Let these groups of three pentagons dry so that they are fairly rigid, then fasten all of the sides together with strips of pasted paper so as to get the final solid figure. Use plenty of paper in the coating so that the wire is safely covered and no sharp ends are able

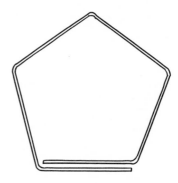

Figure 29.   Wire pentagon for geometrical garden house.

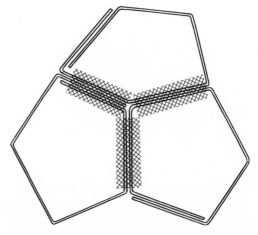

Figure 30.   Fasten the pentagons together three at a time with pasted paper.

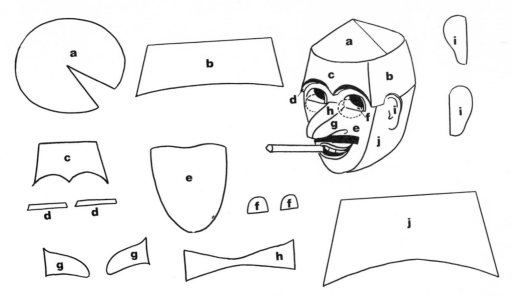

Figure 31. BUILDING UP A CARNIVAL MASK FROM CARDBOARD CUT-OUTS
The top of the head (a) is bent round to make a shallow cone, and (b) and (j) bent round to form the back of the head.

to come through. You should now have a kind of large openwork ball that stands on one of its faces. With wirecutters or tin snips cut away the bare wires, leaving a doorway, and turn in the sharp ends with pliers, covering them with pasted paper for further protection.

Now you can cover the structure with paper, leaving the doorway free and any openings that you want for windows. A good way to make windows that are rainproof is to cut a suitable pentagon from transparent plastic sheet, the kind sold for making plastic greenhouses. Fasten this to the edges of one of the holes with gummed cloth tape (don't use Sellotape or Scotch Tape as it is difficult to cover this with paper so as to make a watertight joint).

If you cut out pentagons in fairly thick cardboard to fit the holes, your construction will have sharper, more modern lines. Glue these to the paper wrapped round the wire framework.

Now cover the whole structure, except the windows and door, with about ten layers of pasted newspaper and one layer of white paper (this can be lining quality wallpaper, or old typing paper, or any other white paper you happen to have. Authors could well consider using the manuscripts of published books!). Put another layer of white paper inside, and be sure to cover the framework of the door with plenty of paper wrapped round from outside to inside to give a soft curve to the doorway. Now let the whole structure dry, sandpaper any very rough bits, make sure that there are no spiky bits of wire poking out anywhere, and give the whole capsule several coats of gloss paint. (Again, let the paint soak in to waterproof the paper.) If you wish, coat the whole structure with varnish as a further protection, particularly on the bottom face that may be left on wet grass.

CARNIVAL MASKS

The enormous masks used in Mardi Gras and other carnivals can be made by making a framework that will hold itself in shape and then covering it with paper. In this case you will have to decide on the kind of mask you want to make and then, preferably on paper, work out the main planes of the face. Figure 31 illustrates the method for a large

Groucho Marx face. The aim should be simplicity of construction and a certain boldness in design, so do not be too complicated in your analysis of the planes. When you have worked out the best combination of flat shapes, draw these onto cardboard and cut them out. (If you are really concerned to make a complicated mask, I suggest that you make a small model first, in thin cardboard, and then enlarge the patterns when you have got it exactly right.)

Using gummed paper tape, stick the cardboard shapes together. Most masks made in this way will hold themselves up in shape as soon as the tape is dry, but if you have any difficulty make a large loop of wire and use this to hold the head in shape (Figure 32). Now proceed to cover the whole head

Figure 32. Wire support for large heads. The joints are tied with wire.

with layers of pasted paper in the usual way, paint it to suit yourself and varnish it heavily inside and out. Details like the position of eyeholes and so on should be fairly simple, but a glance at Figure 51 on page 72 may give you a few useful ideas.

FURNITURE

While not many of us could make furniture with the grace and complexity displayed by such masters of papier mâché as Henry Clay or Jennens and Bettridge, there is no reason why the home craft worker should not turn out very attractive and useful pieces of furniture with that extra aura of originality that comes from hand workmanship for one's own pleasure. The furniture so made can be just as strong as commercial articles, and has the immense advantage of lightness and portability.

In many ways the lightness of papier mâché hastened its departure from the fashionable scene. In the early 1800s, the best time for papier mâché furniture, fashions in clothes mirrored the lightness and elegance of the furniture. Muslin dresses were the in-thing, worn with the simplest and lightest underwear, and, as the *Lady's Monthly Museum* put it in 1803: 'a dress may now be made so exceedingly fine and thin, that it may be carried in a pocket-book or conveyed by the two-penny post to any part of the town'. Those who were shocked by the micro-skirt or hot pants might like to reflect on the situation in 1802–3 when the same magazine described 'a party of high-bred young ladies, who were dressed or rather undressed in all the nakedness of the mode ... they might have passed for so many statues very lightly shaded with drapery'.

Men's dress of the time, though not so exiguous, was tight and cut close to the body, so that any fashionable party of ladies and gentlemen around 1800–1820 would have presented a very slim-line look, very suitable for the elegant papier mâché furniture of the period.

The 1830's came, and with them a reaction against the 'immodest' dress of Regency times. Ladies put on their stays and petticoats again, and skirts swelled out, first with the extra petticoats, then with the bustle, and by 1850 with hoops to hold them out like a balloon. The men laid aside their tight breeches and neat cutaway coats and took to trousers and frock coats with wide skirts to them. Every time somebody moved in the new fashionable gatherings, one of the delicate papier mâché chairs or tables went flying, and in any case the lady of the time needed a chair with room for two — herself and her skirt. The little chairs were sent to the bedrooms or the nursery, and the delicate folding tables remained folded permanently, out of harm's way.

Papier mâché now recommends itself especially for furniture that is unusual in design, and for pieces that would have to be carved by hand if they were made of wood, but can be moulded from paper.

Stool from the Congo

Figure 33 shows a design, based on an original stool from the Congo. The carver was an unknown genius who flourished in the village of Buli among the Luba tribe.

Figure 33. Buli stool.

You can modify the design to suit yourself, of course, and change the type of figure. The large hands and head in the original stool tend to emphasise the subservient pose : the stool was made for a chief to sit on, and the figure is meant to show a proper respect. If you feel that the idea of a woman holding up a stool is too obviously a product of male chauvinist piggery (as of course it is !) by all means make the supporter a man or a monkey.

To make the stool, the supporting figure is modelled in Plasticine or clay. You can save a certain amount of material by using a large bottle or other solid object in the middle, not for strength but just to fill out the volume. Cover this with laminated paper. Use plenty of paper if you intend that people should actually sit on the stool – 12 layers would be none too few. Cut along the sides to release the original model and paste the two halves together with strips of paper. If you want extra strength, place pieces of wood or wire inside the model before you put it together. These are used for reinforcement as explained later.

To make the seat, cut out a number of layers of paper in the right circular shape, and paste them together, again using about 12 layers. If you leave this to dry without any support or clamp it should warp into a concave shape, and with luck this will be just the right shape that you need. If it shows signs of warping too far press it between two heavy boards until it is quite dry. Make the base similarly.

If you want to reinforce the supporting figure for extra strength, make a hole in the top of one of the fingers in each hand, and a small hole in the head somewhere in the headdress. Through the holes in the fingers pour in epoxy resin, mixed with the correct catalyst as described on pages 21–22, until the figure is full. The hole in the head is to let air out so that the liquid resin will penetrate right up the body and head. Now leave the figure for the resin to set hard. It will be much heavier than a hollow papier mâché figure, of course, but very strong. If you want to compromise between strength and weight, make holes in the fingers as explained before, pour in *some* liquid resin, and tilt the figure to and fro so that the interior gets a good layer of resin all over. Keep the figure moving from time to time until the resin is completely set, otherwise it will all drain down to the bottom.

Now fasten the figure to the seat and the base, using thin screws, and paint the whole stool. If you want a wood finish like the original, give the stool a coat of white emulsion paint followed by a good wood varnish stain. If necessary coat the finished stool with polyurethane clear varnish for added lustre and damp-proofing. In the original stool the figure is decorated in black at certain points.

Coffee Table

Figure 34 shows another furniture construction, designed by the author, in which alternate male and female figures hold up a coffee table top (which at least equalises the duties of the sexes!). The figures, one of

Figure 34. Coffee table design based on laminated figures.

each, were made in Plasticine, taking care to model them very thin and starved-looking — painfully thin arms and legs, narrow bodies, an absurdly constricted wasp-waist for the female figure, and so on. This was to allow for the thickness of laminated paper that would be added to every dimension. A properly proportioned model in Plasticine would have come out very fat and clumsy by the time the layers of paper had been added. As the figures are only about 18 in. high, the thickness of paper makes quite a difference to the shape.

The models were laminated with 10 layers of paper, which was then removed from the Plasticine model in the usual way. While the first two figures were being developed from this stage, the Plasticine was repaired and smoothed and another pair of figures started.

Before uniting the halves of the figures, a skeleton armature in wire was made and placed inside the papier mâché. The halves were then put together with pasted paper strips, and two layers of white paper pasted over the whole of each figure.

When all four figures were ready and dry, the heads were cut off. The bodies were filled with epoxy resin, mixed with catalyst, through the neck, and the heads also filled with the resin. Before the resin finally set, a wire was pushed into the interior of each head and down into the neck to hold the figures together once more. One or two pieces of pasted paper on the neck concealed any marks of cutting. Once the epoxy resin was set, the figures were sandpapered and finished with gesso to a smooth surface.

The table top and the supporting base that connects the legs together at the ankle could be made from papier mâché entirely, but were actually, in this construction, made from plywood cut to the right shapes with a coping saw and then covered with one or two layers of paper to give smooth edges. The joins between the uplifted hands and the table top were made by boring two small holes in the plywood at each corner, and passing wire through these: this was then twisted around the hands and concealed with pasted paper. A similar join was made at the ankles to fix the base board. All this extra paper is another reason for starting off with very thin models.

Finally the whole table was varnished with a wood stain varnish and polyurethane clear varnish. Those who prefer a wood-grained top could use veneer over the ply-wood, or even work with a piece of ready-veneered plywood, although concealing the fastenings of the figures may be a little more difficult in this case.

CHAPTER 7

Papier Mâché for Stage Work

Everyone who has been connected with stage or pageant work, whether with children, amateurs, or even professionals working on a low budget, knows the enormous difficulty of getting the appropriate props, all those bits and pieces of furniture and stage dressing that are needed for a good production. There are usually artists who can be approached for the backdrops and scenery, and home dressmakers who will help out with costumes, but the stage furniture and other properties are hard to find. Hiring is expensive, and all too often the hired props show all the signs of constant use and are very shabby. Borrowing is full of hazards. Mrs Robinson may be crazy enough to lend you her genuine Ming vase for the Chinese scene, but are you crazy enough to accept it, having seen the leading man fall over his feet into the furniture at the last rehearsal?

Apart from the danger of breakage, there is the question of weight. Scene-shifters dislike heavy furniture and cannot be expected to get it off stage either quickly or quietly.

This is where papier mâché comes in. Papier mâché pieces are light, almost unbreakable, and can be turned out by any competent craft worker for almost no expense. Indeed, one of the revivals of the art of papier mâché arose during the reign of Louis XIV of France, for making the elaborate scenic devices and furniture for theatrical productions at the court of Versailles.

FOOD AND CONTAINERS

Simple props like fruit, meat, pies and so on can be made very lifelike in papier mâché pulp, and have the advantage that they are not only non-perishable but can be thrown about the stage without damage to themselves or the actors. If you want such things to throw *at* people, make them in laminated paper on a Plasticine mould, so that they are hollow – solid pulp is rather hard and heavy and being hit with a papier mâché pulp banana is almost as painful as being hit with a real one.

Bowls, pots, tankards and so on can be made of laminated paper and decorated in the appropriate style. Again working on a Plasticine mould is best. For really large pots it is best to use the same technique as for the dragon in pages 43–44, making rings of cardboard glued together, starting with smaller rings for the base and building up the size to swell the shape of the pot (see Figure 35), then making smaller rings for the neck. Paste strips of paper vertically down the series of rings to hold them together, hanging the pot from a string in its base to allow it to dry without collapsing like a concertina. When it is thick enough add handles, if required, made of ropes of paper dipped in white glue. Paint the whole pot in gesso or emulsion paint and varnish. The pot illustrated in Figure 35 would be suitable for Biblical scenes such as Isaac meeting Rebekah at the well (Genesis 24,

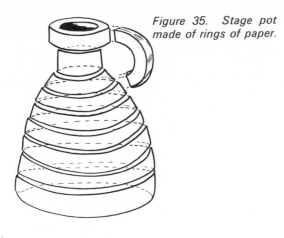

Figure 35. Stage pot made of rings of paper.

newspaper, followed by painting in the normal way. If you are in a hurry (and what stage designer was ever *not* in a hurry?) you can speed up drying by placing a small heater under the hollow 'rock'. Watch out carefully for signs of scorching, however.

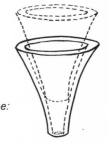

Figure 36. Stage palm tree: units for making the trunk.

15–21), and would overcome a lot of difficulties for a children's play presentation, for example, as the pot would be light enough for a small girl and also unbreakable.

MIRRORS

Mirrors are always dangerous things to have on the stage, and may have superstitious actors seriously worried. Quite satisfactory mirrors can be made with a shape made in laminated papier mâché and the 'mirror face' made of metal cooking foil carefully stuck down. If you want a more elaborate mirror, in Baroque style, for instance, you can make a suitable moulding in papier mâché pulp as described in pages 38–39, cover a piece of board with cooking foil, and then glue the moulding round the edges (see Figure 15, page 39). Do not try too hard to get detailed patterns, because they never show up to the audience, just try to create the effect of rich scroll designs. If you are working for TV or films, of course, you can make up pieces of property or furniture in a detailed style suitable for close-up.

SCENE EFFECTS

Rocks and boulders strong enough for the actors to sit on, but light and fairly quiet to move, can be made by shaping wire netting (chicken wire) roughly into the right form and covering it with several sheets of pasted

Palm trees, inseparable from desert islands and the exotic South, can be conveniently made by moulding a number of cones with slightly flared bases (see Figure 36) in laminated papier mâché. The bottom one is glued or screwed to a base board that can be coated with glue and dusted with sand, or whatever the ground is supposed to be, and the rest are piled one into another to make the trunk of the tree. The top cone is used to support leaves cut out from green paper or thin cardboard. You can either glue all the cones together, or make the tree in two parts that will come apart again for storage. The use of separate cones allows you to give the trunk a graceful lean before you glue the parts together. If you want coconuts, make them of laminated papier mâché.

ELABORATE DECORATION

Many simple objects can be decorated with papier mâché so that they look, at least on the stage, far more elaborate and expensive than they really are. For example, if you have a plain kitchen table you can convert it into an antique Jacobean carved piece of furniture by applying 'carvings' shaped out of papier mâché pulp stuck onto a paper backing and painted with wood stain. If you paste the paper backing onto the table you can remove it with a little water without any damage to the wood.

Similarly, if you want three jewelled caskets for Portia in *The Merchant of Venice*, get hold of three plain wooden boxes of the right size (or even cardboard ones if your budget is very limited). Make panels of 'richly carved' papier mâché pulp to fit the sides and tops of the boxes: if you are satisfied with simple bold effects it looks better on the stage and you can make all the mouldings from about two patterns. Paste on the decorations and paint the boxes. The gold casket can be painted with a gold aerosol spray: a few pieces of foil-backed paper or Dutch metal (a cheap, alloy substitute for gold leaf) will improve the lustre under the stage lights. The silver casket can similarly be sprayed and the highlights picked out with small pieces of cooking foil. For the lead casket use aluminium paint and give it a thin wash over with varnish coloured blue. Then stick on glass 'jewels', and Portia has her three caskets.

'BREAKABLE' OBJECTS

Papier mâché is also most useful for pieces of property that have to be maltreated during a play. A simple case, common in farces, is the hat that gets sat on. If you are doing several performances, it is almost impossible to make the hat look wearable after it has been sat on once or twice. On the other hand, a hat made of laminated paper can be made up for each performance, and will crush with convincing destruction. (Actually papier mâché is very useful for stage hats of all kinds, and my wife and I have, before now, provided a whole cast with hats with no more raw material than cornflake packets, newspaper, paste and paint.)

Another type of 'breakable' prop is papier mâché 'china' that can be used over and over again for accidents on the stage. The Chinese Buddha statue in Plate 7 and Figure 37 was created for several performances of Peter Shaffer's *Black Comedy*. The comedy in this one-act play is that, although the stage lights are on, the cast are supposed to be people groping about in the dark during a

Figure 37. Breakable Buddha for stage work. The joints have been exaggerated for the picture.

power failure. At one point a priceless Chinese statue, borrowed surreptitiously by the hero to impress a visitor, is knocked over and smashed. Obviously the piece has to look like a priceless Chinese statue, but equally obviously no one can afford to smash even copies of such things at every performance. The answer was to make the statue in laminated papier mâché, carefully decorated to look authentic, but so made that the statue would fall apart into jagged-edged pieces if knocked over. A 'glass-smash' effect behind the scenes completed the illusion.

The head was moulded separately, with rather a long neck so that it would sit comfortably in the neck of the body portion without being fixed. The body was made on a Plasticine mould, finished and painted in the normal way, and then sawn into three detachable fragments with a coping saw. By choosing the cuts carefully, it was made possible to balance the parts together in a fairly stable way for the first part of the play, while as soon as the statue was knocked off the table it broke apart very realistically, into four pieces.

LARGE STAGE PROPS

The rigidity of papier mâché makes it very suitable for making large pieces of stage furniture or scenery where wood and other materials would be too heavy and clumsy. Fountains, well-heads, and so on can easily be made in paper, and will look very realistic if decorated with 'carving' in paper pulp. Figure 38 shows the construction of a 'marble' well-head suitable for a play such as *Antony and Cleopatra*. With a little care it can look quite authentic while only weighing a few pounds. The framework is made in cardboard or thin hardboard (Masonite), the joins being made with cloth tape and glue. If the joints are made hinged, the well-head can be folded up for storage. The rim of the well is cardboard folded over at the edge, and the carved supports and heads are made in papier mâché pulp — one mould will do for each if you have time to get the several supports and heads dry. The well-head is painted in very pale gray paint, and the veins of marble sketched in with a small brush in dull pink and darker gray. If the play requires actors to sit on the edge of the well, or lean over it with their weight on the rim, it can be made stronger by laminating

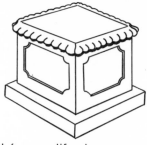

Figure 39. Plinth for stage statues made from a box covered with papier mâché.

Using papier mâché, even life-size statues can be introduced on the stage. If the statue has a plinth, make this out of a wooden box of about the right size, building up a rim with cardboard glued on and making scrolls, etc., in pulped paper (see Figure 39). The statue is best made on a wood and wire armature, which need not be very elaborate as the weight of the paper will not be excessive even when it is wet. Shape your armature roughly to the pose of the required statue (Figure 40); rough out the shape with wire mesh, tacked onto the armature with staples into the wood or wire ties. Drape this mesh with scrim dipped in wall plaster (not plaster of Paris which sets too fast, but builders' plaster like Keene's cement, Sirapite or U.S. patching plaster) made into a thin paste. This will set hard in a few hours.

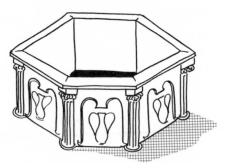

Figure 38.   Folding well-head for stage work.

layers of paper over the edges, without adding unduly to the weight.

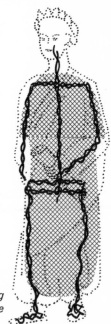

Figure 40.   Wire and netting armature for a classical statue for stage use.

If the statue is of the classical kind with flowering draperies, a toga, or similar garments, make these with newspaper dipped in thin paste made up to a cream with plaster of Paris. This hardens faster than the paste alone but slower than the plaster alone, and should give you time to shape the folds of the drapes. Don't try to be too elaborate — remember that you can always suggest some of the folds by shading when you paint the statue. Finally build up the detail, such as the face and hands, in papier mâché pulp. Gray emulsion paint makes quite a good finish for such a statue: as I have said, go over it (when you have seen it in something like the stage lighting) with darker gray paint putting in shadows to accentuate modelling where this seems to be necessary. If the statue is supposed to be bronze use gold spray paint and put in patches of verdigris in greenish-blue emulsion paint or poster colour.

PUPPETS

At the other end of the scale from full-size statues come puppets, an old but still popular branch of the theatrical family. Puppets are very suitable for construction in papier mâché, and are ideal projects for children to learn the practical sides both of papier mâché making and dramatic presentation.

The simplest type of puppet, very suitable for the beginner and also often extremely effective in appearance, is made as follows. Take a piece of Plasticine and roll it into the rough shape of an egg. The size is not really important, but if the puppets are to be used together, for a class performance, for instance, it is a good thing for them to be all the same size. A little larger than a large hen's egg is about right. This is small enough to handle easily, even in a child's hand, but large enough to prevent the detail from being too finicky. Take another piece of Plasticine and stick it on to the small end of the egg to make a neck, press the thumbs in about halfway up the egg to make sockets for the eyes, and pull out the chin to make it

less receding. Shape the nose from a small piece of Plasticine and stick it on the face. For these simple models ears are not really necessary, but they can be expressed as simple lumps in the right places if desired. The result should be rather skull-like but recognisably a head and neck.

Now coat the head with about six layers of newspaper dipped in paste: for children cellulose paste is undoubtedly the best material, as it will not mark their clothes if they drop paste over themselves. If several types of paper are available, this makes it easier to tell when layers are complete (see pages 23–24). Tear the paper into small pieces so that there will not be unsightly folds and creases on the face. Finish off with a layer of white paper. In every layer, take care to push the paper well into the eye-sockets and around the nose so as not to lose too much shape in the head. Be sure that the neck is adequately covered, as this has to support the head and there is a tendency for the layers to stop short so that the bottom of the neck is weakened. When all the layers are on, put the head aside in a warm place to dry.

When the head is dry it is cut in half between the face and the back of the head (see Figure 41). This allows the Plasticine

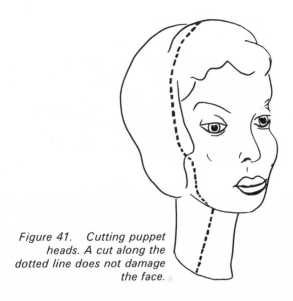

Figure 41. Cutting puppet heads. A cut along the dotted line does not damage the face.

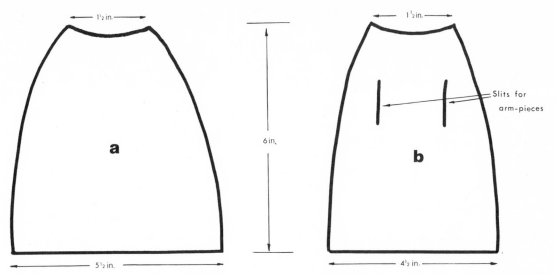

Figure 42. *GLOVE FOR PUPPETS*
(a) back   (b) front.   The sleeves are stitched into the slits at the front.

to be removed but does not damage the face of the puppet. The two halves are peeled off the Plasticine and then stuck together with small pieces of pasted paper (with a little skill some of these can be poked inside, through the neck, to reinforce the join from the inside). Now the head is put to dry again (this drying stage will not take long, as the paper is able to dry from both sides when it is off the Plasticine mould). Give the paper a coat of white emulsion paint or gesso inside and out — the quickest way to coat the inside is to pour a little paint in and move it around by tipping the head from side to side. Finally paint the inside down to the opening of the neck. It is now ready for the features to be painted. Poster colours take well on emulsion paint, but inks or acrylic paints can equally well be used.

Finally varnish the head with clear polyurethane varnish inside and out, and add any details such as hair and beards. Frayed jute, or even string, makes quite good hair. Old woollen sweaters and similar things can be unravelled to make splendid curly hair. This can be stuck on with clear glue. Alternatively, short hair styles can be made by sticking on small pieces of fur fabric or even flock-sprayed wallpaper.

The puppet heads made in this way are very suitable for glove and hand puppets. Figure 42 gives an elementary pattern for the glove portion of the puppet. Note that the back is larger than the front to allow for the curvature of the hand. Doll-makers' felt or any other scraps of material can be pressed into service for the bodies, and the neck of the puppet head is sewn onto the neck of the 'glove' (it may be necessary to make the holes in the neck of the papier mâché head with a bradawl or other spiked instrument for ease of sewing, for if the papier mâché has been made properly it is very tough). Obviously the costume can be much more elaborate than the simple type in the drawing, which was intended for children to make without help.

Puppets made in this elementary way are very pleasing, and can be made to have quite expressive faces with a little care in painting. However, the lack of modelling in the face makes them all look very much alike, and most people having made one or two of such puppet heads will want to go on to a type with more character.

There are two ways of doing this. One is to model the head directly in papier mâché pulp. Roll a tube in cardboard about three inches long and wide enough to insert the index finger comfortably. It can be stuck with gummed paper. Using this as the neck, add paper pulp (see page 34 for the method) to form a rough head shape. Exaggerate the features at this stage, and do not try to form fine detail like eyelids, just concentrate on the overall proportions of the head. Now stand the head to dry fairly hard but still damp — you can make a simple stand for it by sticking an old pencil or used-up ball point pen in a lump of Plasticine, and using this to hold the neck tube.

When it is getting harder, and has shrunk somewhat, work over the pulp with a clay tool, small knife blade, or other tool to form the details of the features (the choice of tools is always a matter for the individual worker: I always use small electrical screwdrivers for modelling, but I do not expect that they would suit other craftsmen). The final smoothing of the head, after the pulp is completely dry, can be carried out with small pieces of sandpaper, sandpaper files that are sold for fine work, or even manicure files, in emergency. Now coat the head with white paint or gesso and paint in the features.

Drying papier mâché pulp takes a lot longer than the laminated material, so give your model ample time in a warm place before you paint it. If you coat it with gesso while the inside is still moist, the pulp will contract as it dries and pull away from the gesso coating, which will then either crack or wrinkle. A good way of telling whether pulp is still moist, when it is warm, is to lay it on a piece of mirror. If the mirror clouds over, even a little, put the model back to dry some more.

Papier mâché pulp is not always the easiest material to shape, and if you are more used to working with clay or Plasticine you can use these materials to model your puppet heads. For those who have never tried this type of modelling before, Figure 43 gives a sequence of operations that may make the job easier: the idea is to start off with a kind of skull shape in Plasticine, and gradually clothe it with 'flesh'. This is somewhat easier than

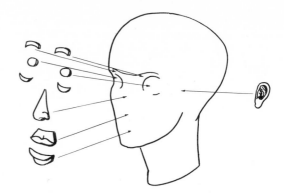

Figure 43. Building up a face. Put the eyes on first, then mould the eyelids over them.

starting with a lump of Plasticine and trying to introduce detailed modelling immediately, because with the 'skull' method you can concentrate on one aspect at a time. If you want ideas for faces, study people you meet during the day and try to work out what shapes give them their characteristic expression, deep-set eyes or shallow ones, high cheek-bones or pendulous cheeks, and so on, and you will soon be able to make your little pieces of Plasticine form a whole gallery of faces.

When you have made your head, with a good length of neck for attaching it to the clothes, you must cast it in plaster. There are notes on this process in Chapter Three, but the following quick summary may help.

Find a box or container that will hold the Plasticine head with about $\frac{1}{4}$ in. or more all round (Figure 44). Plastic containers used for packaging food such as mushrooms are quite suitable, as the container need not be very strong as long as it is watertight. Mix up plaster of Paris to a thick cream in sufficient quantity to fill about half the box or container. Shake the plaster to remove bubbles, and tap the bottom of the container to make them come to the surface. You can get rid of the bubbles there by pricking them or blowing on them. Now pick up your Plasticine head by pushing a matchstick or cocktail stick into the upper surface, and put it into the plaster. Move it around a little to make sure that no bubbles are trapped underneath it, and then hold it so that it is exactly half immersed in the plaster. Soon the plaster will thicken and get warm, and you should be able to feel when it is safe to let the Plasticine head go. Allow the plaster to set thoroughly in a warm place.

Now with a drill and countersink bit, or with the blade of a knife, carve two little conical pits in the plaster on either side of the head. This makes sure that the other half of the mould will fit exactly, as it will have two little 'pegs' which correspond with the pits. Coat the plaster with some kind of lubricant to make sure that the other half of the mould will not stick. Soap is quite suitable for this: use a thick solution made either from soap flakes or by dissolving a piece of toilet soap in hot water. Alternatively you can use petroleum jelly rubbed over the plaster, or even spray the plaster with penetrating oil from an aerosol can.

Now make up some more plaster and pour it over the upper part of the head and the lower mould. If you want to be quite sure of avoiding bubbles in the plaster, paint a layer of plaster over the head with a soft brush before you pour the rest. Let this set, and then carefully prise the two halves of the mould apart and remove the Plasticine head. You may have to tear open the box in which you have made the moulds.

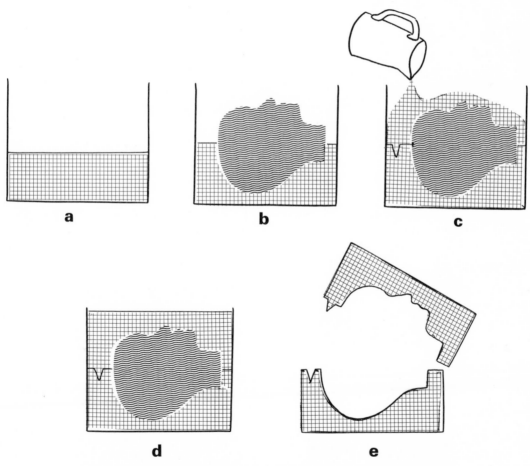

Figure 44. MAKING MOULDS FROM A PLASTICINE HEAD
(a) Box half filled with plaster   (b) back of head positioned   (c) pouring top half of mould
(d and e) the completed mould.

Now dry the moulds carefully and give them both a coat of varnish, copal or polyurethane. A lot of this will be absorbed by the plaster: if you get an eggshell gloss finish the coating is thick enough, but if the inside of the mould is still matt when the varnish has dried, give the plaster another coat.

When the varnish has dried, oil the mould with cooking oil, lubricating oil, or melted petroleum jelly (Vaseline). Now you can mould pasted paper against the insides of the two halves of the mould.

To get the sharpest impression, the paper must be very thin and soft. If you are using newspaper, tear it into very small pieces and soak these in paste, rubbing them down well into the details of the moulds. I find that cleansing tissues (Kleenex or similar) work very well: they tear too easily to be pasted with a brush, but if they are rapidly dipped in water and then into cellulose paste they can be squeezed down into the moulds and rubbed into the detailed hollows of the plaster. Put in a good layer of tissues, about $\frac{1}{8}$ in thick, and let them dry a little, pushing them down with the finger while they are still damp so as to get a good impression. Then paste over inside the layers of tissues and put on two or three layers of paper. Run up over the sides of the mould so as to keep the thickness even: this surplus is cut off later. Now put the filled moulds away to dry — this may take some time, as the tissues hold water tenaciously.

When the paper is quite dry, before you remove it from the mould, trim the edges with a craft knife so that the paper is no higher than the sides of the mould. Then extract the two halves and stick them together with small pieces of pasted paper along the join. You should have an exact copy of your Plasticine model which will take only a small amount of smoothing to finish off. Cover it with paint or gesso in the usual way (the tissues will tend to absorb more than an ordinary paper surface) and paint in the features.

If the face you are making is fairly normal, with no very exaggerated features, it is best to make the division between the moulds run as if from ear to ear so that the face is all in one piece and there are no pieces of jointing paper running over it. However, if the face has some undercut parts, for instance a witch with a hooked nose and long chin, these would not come out of a plaster mould undamaged, and you will have to make the moulds so that the join runs halfway across the face (see Figure 45). Although this also means that you will have to paste the jointing paper over the face, this does not matter so much, as faces with undercut parts can usually be rather 'craggy' in other ways.

MARIONETTES
Marionettes can be made by very similar techniques to those suggested for puppets, except that the body will have to be made of joined pieces. The heads are produced by any of the processes described above, except that instead of a hollow neck they should have a solid one with a wire ring or screw eye set in, for jointing to the body. If you are modelling in pulp just fix a ring in the neck before the pulp dries: if you are using laminated paper a piece of cork or wood can be set into the neck with glue, to hold the wire.

Make your marionette skeleton out of twisted wire: thin wire twisted up gives a better surface to model on to than thicker wire with a smooth surface. Figure 46 gives some suggestions for the wire shapes. In the legs and arms double loops are made at one end of a piece of wire, and single loops on the adjoining ones, so that the single loop can be placed between the double ones making a strong hinge. These hinges are tied with strong nylon thread. At the knee make a little projecting piece of wire to prevent the shin from bending forwards: this makes the action of the marionette far more realistic.

Cover the wires with strips of pasted paper wound round and round and modelled to the desired shape. The body can be covered with larger pieces, making sure that the movement at the waist is not interfered with. If you want a really good finish, model over the

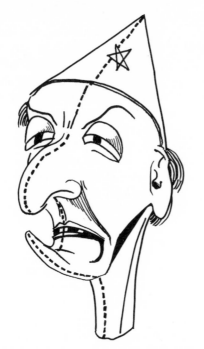

Figure 45. How to remove a puppet head from the mould when there are undercut details.

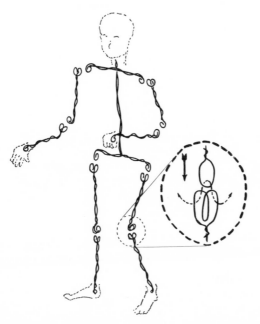

Figure 46. Wire armature for marionettes. The single loops fit between the double loops and are tied.

layers of paper with well-rubbed paper pulp, and then sandpaper the finished model when dry.

PUNCH AND JUDY

Those who take an interest in hand puppets may be familiar with these characters, the actors in the oldest puppet show still surviving in anything like its original form, but it is a sad fact that there are very few of the traditional Punch and Judy shows in existence. Once a common sight in English streets at any period from the eighteenth century up to about 1914, the shows gradually declined in numbers and moved away from the streets to the holiday beaches and fairs, and eventually ceased to compete at all with the cinema and TV for people's attention.

Yet Punch and his companions in the show are part of a very long and important theatrical progression. The character of Punch himself, cunning, violent, completely amoral, and therefore always coming out on top of any situation, starts with the cunning slaves who twist the plots of Greek and Roman comedy. As *Punchinello* he appears in the Renaissance Italian commedia dell'arte (hence his English name), and he came to England about 1662 as a puppet character. If one wants to be solemn about Punch (and a lot of people have been terribly solemn about him), one could draw parallels between Punch, who scores off everyone including the Devil, and what Jung called the Trickster archetype who occurs in folklore all over the world.

If the history of puppetry interests you, you will find the background of Punch a fascinating study. I shall merely describe the characters of the traditional show as an example of the manufacture and dressing of hand puppets.

The characters in the most commonly presented versions of the play are Punch himself, his unfortunate wife Judy, their baby, the Doctor, the hangman Jack Ketch (named after a real executioner in England who died in 1686), and the Devil. Joey the Clown and a clacking crocodile rather like the one in *Peter Pan* are often added to the cast list, and there is always Toby the Dog, although this part was often played by a real performing dog, much to the pleasure of the children in the audience. There are other characters that have been introduced, such as Pretty Polly and the Courtier, but these make the performance longer. Details of the show were always changing because it was essentially a street entertainment: if the audience were large and enthusiastic, the showman would put in extra characters and show off his skill with the puppets: if the audience were thin, or the weather looked bad, the showman would go through the minimum of performance and hurry to make his collection at the end.

Figure 47 gives sketches of the faces and costumes of most of the characters in the traditional show.

Mr Punch himself is always dressed in a rather showy red and yellow costume with a gown and ruff, which derived from the dress of Elizabethan clowns. His triangular hat with the tassel, a 'sugar-loaf hat', is similar to the military hats used on both sides of the Atlantic around 1780–90. His face is traditionally ugly, with a long nose almost meeting a long chin, and he has a hump-back which is usually suggested by a small conventionalised hump in the back of his gown. As he carries a stick which he uses enthusiastically on almost every other member of the cast, his hands have to be accessible to the showman's fingers so that he can pick it up and wield it realistically. The book jacket shows a version of Punch. The head was made from papier mâché moulded over Plasticine, and painted with gesso and acrylic colours. The hat was moulded in one piece with the head, as it does not have to be removable and a moulded hat is less likely to come off by accident. The legs and feet are dummies fastened on the outside of the 'glove' part of the puppet: for ease of construction they are made in papier mâché pulp and sewn onto the cloth legs of the costume.

Judy has a face like that of her husband, and is traditionally dressed in a gown with an apron and a mob cap, the frilly cap favoured by ladies around 1780–90. In the early Punch and Judy shows she was a

Figure 47. Punch, Judy, the Baby, and Toby the Dog.

fighting (and nagging) character, but recent versions have made her rather more long-suffering. The *Baby* is just a roll of clothes with a papier mâché head and hands; it can have some family resemblance to its parents as in Figure 47.

The *Doctor* is an eighteenth century figure with bands at his neck and a long gown which helps to hide the showman's hand. He could, of course, be modernised and have a white coat and stethoscope, or even an operating gown.

Jack Ketch should be dressed in black and preferably in the style of the eighteenth century, with knee breeches and a long coat. A black mask helps to make him look more sinister and more like the traditional executioner, although such masks were not in fact worn very often. The *Devil* can be as grotesque as you like to make him, with claws on his hands, horns on his head, and either claws or hooves on his feet (which are dummies, like Mr. Punch's feet). Red is a good colour for the Devil, but black looks better in contrast to Mr Punch's red and yellow gown, and you can save the red for details like the Devil's mouth, hands, and horns, or put red flame-like fringes on his gown.

Unless you happen to have a performing dog of small size, *Toby* will have to be made: he is just a papier mâché head and front paws mounted in a simple brown glove. Other characters can be designed according to the version of the play you want to use — for example, *Pretty Polly* is a typical dumb glamour girl and does not even have working arms and legs. She is just a doll on a stick (which enables her to have a waistline, a thing that no genuine glove puppet can have).

STAGE COSTUMES

Apart from the collapsible hat mentioned earlier, papier mâché can find uses for the more rigid parts of many stage costumes. For instance, laminated papier mâché will produce light, strong pieces of armour, or helmets, very suitable for historical plays.

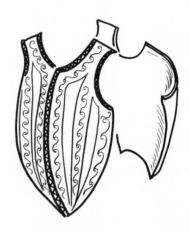

Figure 48.   Spanish helmet and armoured cuirass.

Figure 48 shows a Spanish helmet, backplate and breast-plate of the period of the Spanish Armada.

The armour plates are shaped by cutting out wire mesh to about the right shape, and then modelling these pieces of wire, preferably over the actors who are going to wear the armour. The mesh is then covered on both sides with layers of pasted paper until it has been built up to shape, and the final metallic finish obtained either with metallic paint or foil-covered paper stuck to the papier mâché.

The helmet centre is shaped first on a bowl of about the right size, in pasted paper, but removed from the bowl while it is still slightly damp. At this stage it can be fitted to

69

the head of the actor who is to wear it, and then left standing somewhere to dry before the crest and brim are attached. The helmet is finished exactly as the armour, with paint or foil.

Another piece of costume for which papier mâché is very suitable is a mermaid's tail. Mermaids in plays and similar productions tend to have tails that are either far too heavy and rigid, so that the girl looks and feels as if she is shut up in the lower half of a mummy case, or the tail is just a tight skirt with fish scales painted on it, so that there is always a sharp bend where the knees come.

The paper tail is based on the dragon's tail shown in Chapter four. It is made up of rings of laminated papier mâché connected together so that the tail has a smooth curve without a kink at the knees, but can still move slightly in a sinuous way suitable for a half-fish character.

Make up a number of rings of paper (see Figure 49) of steadily decreasing size, starting just below the hips of the mermaid and working down to the ankles. The top part of the tail, at the hips, is best made as a short piece of cloth skirt painted to match the rest of the tail, so that the actress can sit down comfortably. Make the rings about 9 in

Figure 49. Mermaid's tail. The top section is a short skirt.

deep, and use around four layers of paper. The edges should be scalloped or cut jaggedly to suggest scales. Make a tail for the last ring, leaving room for the feet to hide behind it.

Now connect the rings together like the dragon tail, except that stronger fasteners should be used, two to each segment. This will hold the tail together, but if the actress moves her legs the tail will follow their movement, so that she can built up one or two gestures, a slow waggle or an indignant swish, to suit the situation.

CHAPTER 8

Masks

Laminated papier mâché is peculiarly suitable for making masks of all kinds. Masks need to be strong to stand up to wear and weather, not too thick or clumsy, and above all light, if they are to be worn. The method of manufacture must allow for any kind of detail, from complete naturalism to the most fantastic grotesques. Papier mâché answers all these requirements admirably.

Putting on a new face to the world has always appealed to people in all parts of the world and at all times. Masks have been the adjuncts of religious ceremonies since at least the thirtieth century B.C. and have carried on this function ever since, either to represent the face of the god superimposed on the face of the priest or actor, or simply to strike terror and awe into the spectators and thus make them more easily convinced of the importance of the ceremony. Guy Fawkes' Day and Hallowe'en masks still have the same purpose, in a vastly watered-down way, and give children the chance, one day in the year, to get their own back on the world and *scare* someone.

As a practical lesson in anthropology there is no better activity than to copy in papier mâché and then decorate a 'primitive' mask. We tend not to pay proper attention to the intricacy and craftsmanship of the ethnic exhibits in museums, perhaps because there are so many. Painting or sketching them teaches us a little more about the detail and skill that has gone into many of them, but an even better way of entering into the real feeling of an ancient or far-away culture is to make a complete copy of such an exhibit. We learn which of the characteristics were

due to the material used — carving in hard wood with soft iron or even stone tools, for instance, encourages a certain simplicity of style — and which were due to the ritual requirements of the society. We begin to feel the emotions that were excited by the masks originally, whether they are the sheer terror expressed in, say, a 'wild man' mask of the warlike and aggressive Kwakiutl tribes of British Columbia, or the grave sense of inevitability in an ancient Greek tragic mask. Masks, in fact, reflect a face of the society that created them — not always a realistic face, but one closely tied to the emotional life of the people.

There are really four basic types of mask, differing in the degree to which they cover the head of the wearer. The simplest mask, the face-mask, covers the face only and is usually held on with elastic or a string passing over the ears and round the back of the head. A face-and-head mask is easier to keep on, and gives the opportunity to change the hairstyle or even the apparent height of the wearer. This device can be extended until the construction is a *tall mask*, often used to represent animal heads, where the wearer's head fits into the neck of the mask, as if in a visor of a helmet, and the actual face of the mask is above. The fourth type is the whole-head mask that gives the greatest scope for variation (see Figure 50).

Within these styles it is possible to change the appearance and even the apparent size of the wearer's face by various devices, as in Figure 51. (1a) shows how to make a mask face larger than the wearer's face, (1b) how to make it smaller. (1c) is another device for

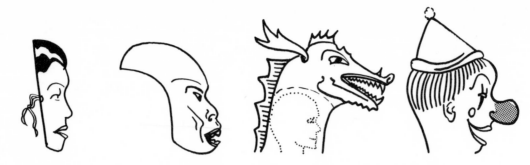

Figure 50.   Face mask, face-and-head, tall mask and full-head mask.

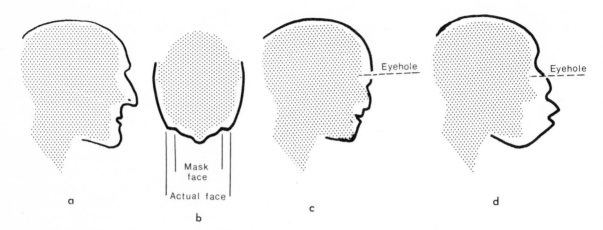

Mask
face

Actual face

a

b

c

Eyehole

Eyehole

d

Figure 51.   Ways to make a mask smaller or larger than the actor's face.

giving the effect of a smaller face, where the mask face is actually below the level of the wearer's eyes and he looks out of eyeholes concealed in the front of the hair. (1d) shows how to make a face considerably larger and more projecting than that of the person inside. All of these tricks are easier to do with a face-and-head or whole-head mask.

To make a mask that fits over the face or head it is best to start with a Plasticine mould and model laminated paper over it. The average head needs a mask about $10\frac{1}{2}$–11 in. high, and about 29–30 in. in circumference if it is a full-head construction. Remember that noses stick out from the face and tend to catch on projecting bits of papier mâché inside the mask quite painfully as you put it on, so be generous in your dimensions for a full-head mask. Simple face-masks can be moulded in Plasticine on a piece of board,

using a block of wood or some similar object in the middle to save Plasticine. Full-head and face-and-head masks can quite conveniently be modelled with Plasticine over a one-gallon plastic pail turned upside-down. This saves pounds of Plasticine and makes the mould lighter to move around.

Lay on the various layers of paper in the usual way for laminated work, putting on about 10 layers for a strong mask. Take care to rub the paper well into hollows such as eye-sockets and beside the nose, so that you do not lose too much detail of the modelling.

When the papier mâché is dry, face-masks can usually be peeled away from the mould, unless there is a great deal of undercutting in the shape (such as a hooked nose, for example). For undercut face masks and other types of mask, cut the paper down the middle

72

of the face and on over the head so as to make two halves that can be removed from the mould. Paste these together with strips of paper inside and outside, and finally give the whole mask a coating of one or two layers of white paper — inside and out, if you are conscientious about your work, but at least on the outside.

Allow the shape to dry and then cut out any holes — mouth, eyes, and so on — required by the design. If the holes are large, like the open mouths of ancient Greek comic masks, for instance, tidy up the edges by pasting small pieces of paper from inside to outside (see Figure 52). At this stage also

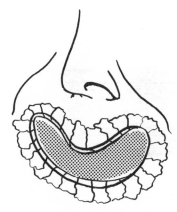

Figure 52.   Smoothing the mouth of a mask with strips of paper.

attach any details — crowns, feathers, strings, beads — in the design that have to be added after moulding. Now paint the mask with two coats of emulsion paint or gesso. When it is dry it is ready for decorating. Finally give the mask a coat of varnish inside and out.

DESIGNS FOR MASKS

You can find designs for masks in great profusion if you go to any good museum with an anthropological section, or in books on primitive art, the theatre and the dance. If you want to make animal faces they can be studied in books, or better, because of the three-dimensional effect, in natural history museums (actual animals in zoos would be ideal to study, if only they kept still rather more). If you want ideas for grotesque masks, study the cover pictures of horror and sci-fi books and magazines. The following descriptions of some of the most important types of ethnic and historical masks are only intended to suggest the vast scope of the subject.

Ancient Greek and Roman Masks

The ancient Greek theatre developed from the dramatic and often orgiastic worship of Dionysus around the sixth century B.C. Because the open-air theatres were so large and spacious, it was difficult for the audiences to see fine shades of acting, and the expressions on an actor's face would be entirely lost except to the front rows of seats. It was necessary, therefore, to make the characters almost literally 'larger than life'. The actors wore masks made of painted canvas, often built up over the head to increase the apparent height of the wearer, and having boldly-drawn, simplified features that expressed the age, sex, and paramount emotions of the character. Eyeholes and nostrils were cut out to allow the actors to see and breathe, and the mouths were often very large, especially in comic roles. The actors soon found that proper design of these large holes could amplify their voices, and the megaphone was born. To keep the large masks on safely as the actors moved about, there was usually a tight-fitting cap inside the structure.

None of these ancient masks is known, although there are some copies in terra cotta and other materials that have been found in Thebes and other centres of Greek civilisation. However, we know quite a lot about the types of character portrayed because most of the traditions of the Greek theatre were taken over later by the Romans. In particular the Roman comedy writer Terence (Publius Terentius Afer, about 184–159 B.C.) borrowed plots and characters from the older Greek writer Menander, and specified with some care the types of mask that should be used for each of the characters in his six comedies. Drawings of these masks exist in very old manuscript copies of Terence's plays, and there is good reason to believe that these are fair representations of the types of mask used in his time. There is a copy of the 'cast-list' from Terence's comedy *Hecyra*, or the Mother-in-Law (which shows that some old jokes are very old indeed). Figure 53 is drawn from a colossal marble tragic mask used to decorate a Roman theatre: it shows the bold dramatic power of these masks.

Such masks can easily be constructed as face-masks or face-and-head, on a Plasticine mould. Do not be afraid to paint them in naturalistic colours as the Romans did (we tend to think of Greek and Roman art as having started as chaste and undecorated as the statues in our museums: in fact they were usually painted quite vividly, but of course the colours have faded and washed away from surviving stone carvings).

Figure 53.   Roman theatre mask.

Primitive Masks

Primitive art suggests something rough and badly finished, but this is far from the reality. Someone has defined primitive art as the high art of low cultures, and while the people who made these objects may have lived very simply, their religious and ceremonial objects were made with loving care and all the skill they could command. After all, if you are making the statue of a rain-god who can increase or destroy your harvest, or a guardian to keep evil spirits out of your hut, you do not work carelessly. The primitive artist is not trying to entertain or fill an idle hour, he is producing things which everybody in the community believes is essential to his well-being.

Many people, children in particular, find much primitive art more immediately appealing than sophisticated western art, especially when they have got over the first sense of 'strangeness' based on their western upbringing. Primitive art deals with the collective expression of experience, and the simple facts of everyday life, far more often than the more individualistic western art.

On the other hand, without any denigration of the primitive workers, it is often fairly easy for the craft-worker of moderate skill to copy ethnic objects. This is often because the primitive artist tends to work with inferior tools on intractable material, while the craft-worker has a far wider choice of tools and materials. As I have said, this kind of copying is one of the best ways to learn something of anthropology. Primitive religion, for example, is difficult to believe or take seriously until one has copied one of the curiously disturbing fetish figures of the western Congo, or the crouching ancestor figures that brood over houses in New Guinea.

A few masks, taken almost at random, are illustrated in Figures 54—60 with some details of construction. Figure 54 is a spirit mask from the Ogooue River region of Gabon. Such masks are worn by men in funeral dances, and they are supposed to represent the spirits of dead female ancestors. The

Figure 54.   Ogooue River mask.

Figure 55.   Timur Batak mask.

Figure 56.   New Guinea fertility mask.

heart-shaped face is very much admired in the Gabon and Congo areas, and much used in masks. The white face is also common for spirit masks — I suppose that in Gabon, right on the Equator, whiteness must seem such an unhealthy colour that it could only relate to the dead.

The mask is best made as a face-and-head. The headdress can either be moulded as part of the Plasticine master copy, or, more easily, made out of a number of crescents of cardboard cut to the right shape, glued together, and then fastened to the mask with pasted paper. The border of the headdress is made with decorative cord.

Figure 55 is also a funeral mask, made by the Timur Batak people of Sumatra. The original was carved from hardwood and decorated with horsehair, and served the melancholy purpose of representing only sons who had died young. This respectful substitute for lying in state is very characteristic of the Batak people, who have possessed a complex and civilised social system for a long time.

The mask is easily produced as a face-mask: the band round the forehead in the original is metal, and could be made with a length of gold-coloured metal ribbon.

Figure 56 is a fertility cult mask from New Guinea. This Tami carving shows the characteristics of the New Guinea mainland — stiff very wooden-looking faces with all the details of eyes, eyebrows, nose, nostrils, tongue and teeth made blocky and geometrical as if in a picture by Léger. A good way to make this mask is in fact to carve out these details in polystyrene foam (Styrofoam) and stick them to the basic face shape with white glue. Do not use a solvent glue, as this will dissolve the polystyrene (see page 21).

Figure 57 is a copy of a carved head from the northern Solomon Islands. These heads represent a personification of the tribal chiefs, and are carried on the prows of the huge war canoes of the Solomons, like a figurehead on a sailing ship. The finish is startlingly smooth and sophisticated, and the decoration in lacquer and pearl shell carried out with great artistry. This model must obviously be made as a full-head mask: the decoration can be cut out of foil-coated paper and stuck on with white glue, unless you want to be really extravagant and paint the designs on the white paint, then coat them with gold leaf or Dutch metal attached with gold size. If so, you will find instructions for this tricky art in pages 81–83. The ears are difficult to mould with the head, and it is better to leave them out of the original Plasticine model and attach them afterwards: they can be made from pieces of cardboard cut out as in Figure 58.

It is interesting that the pearl-shell inlay, so much used by the artist of the Solomons, is also in great demand for ceremonial shields. The shields are made of cane plaited over a bamboo framework, and this is then covered with a layer of black vegetable lacquer which is then decorated with pieces of shell. Although the patterns are different, the technique is very like that used by Alsager and Neville in the nineteenth century for decorating trays with mother-of-pearl. It seems most unlikely that either group of artists, one set in Birmingham, England, and the other in Malaita, Solomon Islands, ever saw one another's work.

Figure 59 is a copy of a mask made by the Iroquois Indians of western New York State. The Iroquois were by far the most highly developed of the north-eastern tribes, with a gift for political organisation that gave a great deal of trouble to the white settlers. Their art shows many affinities with northern Asian art, and these masks are connected with a religion related to Asian *shamanism*, the belief in divinely inspired shamans or priests who have power given to them by their own personal supernatural spirits. The masks are meant to portray such spirits, and this is why they have the staring eyes (made of tin, in this case, from the abandoned cans of the white settlers), the wrinkled brows and the stern and rather ugly expressions, so different from the rather handsome features of the typical Iroquois.

Figure 57.   Solomon Islands canoe figurehead.

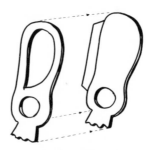

Figure 58.   Constructing the ears for the Solomon Islands mask.

Figure 59.   Iroquois Indian mask. The eyes and nose are tin from a can.

76

When copying this mask it is important to emphasise the wrinkles and folds, and these should be worked over while the papier mâché is still damp to press down the valleys and sharpen the peaks. The eyes and nose are made from pieces cut from a can, as in the original, and the horsetail hair can be rendered quite well with a bunch of nylon bristles.

Figure 60, perhaps the most impressive of the masks I have chosen, is only one of the many striking products of the Kwakiutl tribe of British Columbia. This people have a long tradition, akin to shamanism, of the Wild Man, who is selected from the tribe by a spirit and taken away to acquire supernatural powers. He comes back to the village in a frenzy of magical possession. This story is enacted as a ceremony, and suitable 'wild man' masks created to heighten the excitement and awe of the spectators. The story, although it contains elements of pantomime, is basically a religious ceremony, and the portraits of the shamans' personal spirits must not be handled or interfered with by outsiders. The manufacture of the masks is limited to the elect members of the dance-society who are going to wear them, and often they used to be destroyed after each ceremony to make sure that no one could touch or examine them.

The object in Figure 60 is made as a face-mask, the eyeholes being cut out after drying. The original was decorated with gray horse-hair, but theatrical crepe hair gives just as good a result.

I must emphasise that the few examples I have described represent only a fraction of the interesting and impressive primitive masks that are available for study. Similarly the few details of their significance in the folklore of the people who made them were included merely to give a slight impression of the richness and variety of the social and religious systems that are expressed in primitive art. Finding out all about the anthropology of even one of these masks would lead to researches which could fill this book and more.

Thai Masks

I have separated the masks of Thailand from primitive art because they cannot really be considered as at all primitive, any more than the masks and costumes for Japanese *Noh* plays. The Thai have had a thriving theatre and tradition of courtly dancing for centuries, and have developed an elaborate system of costumes that include whole-head masks of great complexity. Figure 61 shows the details of such a mask, intended to be worn by a devil-dancer, and Plate 9 shows an authentic Thai doll wearing a papier mâché mask, and the same design of mask made full-size. The main part of the mask was made

Figure 60. Kwakiutl shaman mask.

Figure 61. Thai dancer's mask.

in two halves, as already described, but leaving off the crown and the elaborate winged ear decorations. These were cut out of sheets of cardboard built up with one or two layers of white pasted paper, and fixed to the head before painting. The jewels are glass costume jewels stuck to the mask with white glue: they show up better if the paper under them is painted with the appropriate colour (i.e. green patches under the green jewels of the crown, and a red spot of colour under the 'ruby' on the forehead and on the ear pieces).

MASKS FOR DECORATION

Ethnic masks can be made as decorations as well as for wearing. Face-masks can be hung on the wall with no trouble if a suitable string or cord is incorporated in the design, and can be finished off deliberately with a plaque base. The African mask in Plate 10 was made in this way as a wall decoration.

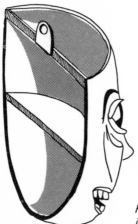

Figure 62. Mask made into a flower pot holder.

Alternatively masks can be converted into unusual and interesting plant-pot holders by fitting a suitable shelf inside them for the pot (see Figure 62). The masks are made with a fair amount of relief, so that they will contain a round pot, but with no top to the head, rather like an inverted bell-shape. The shelf is made with a flat back to fit against the wall, and a front curved to fit the mask about half way down. This shelf can be made of hardboard (Masonite), $\frac{1}{2}$ in. wood, or even several sheets of cardboard glued together. It is glued into the inside of the mask before painting or varnishing. A thin piece of wood across the top of the mask at the back can hold a wire or metal loop or passe partout ring from which to hang the mask. Whichever material is used, wood or cardboard, take extra care that the whole of the mask is varnished thoroughly and that the varnish is waterproof, as pot plants are watered regularly and so will be the mask!

If you want to go further with decoration in the primitive style, try making a series of masks in fairly low relief and with the edges extended outwards to a square or circle. You can cut the edges neatly after the mask is dry. Paste or glue the masks onto the sides and top of wooden boxes — toy boxes, small chests used for storage, or small boxes for holding jewelry and trinkets. A very plain wooden or even cardboard box can be made lively with a series of savage or lofty faces. If you doubt your ability to make a neat wooden box, and have no plain whitewood furniture that you wish to decorate, you can buy small boxes from craft suppliers: many such boxes are available for a small sum for craft workers to cover with shells, and so on.

CHAPTER 9

Paints and Finishes

Apart from the initial design work, there is no more enjoyable stage in a papier mâché project than having a completed and dry model ready for decoration. This is also the stage that allows most scope for personal invention, and I shall not therefore try to give directions for styles or patterns. These will depend on your own tastes, or those of the people to whom you want to give your work, on the kind of model, and on your own special skills.

However, this is a convenient point to summarise the *methods* of painting and finishing papier mâché for various purposes, and the materials that are available. Some notes on this aspect are given earlier in the book as applied to specific projects, but all the methods are assembled in this chapter.

DECORATED PAPERS AND DÉCOUPAGE

The simplest way to cover up a papier mâché model is to stick a layer of decorated paper over it, or cover it with cut-out pictures and shapes.

If the papier mâché is fairly flat you will have no difficulty in covering it smoothly with wallpaper, foil-covered paper or other decorated materials. For foil-covered paper use white glue or a similar washable craft glue so that you can remove any smears of adhesive with a damp cloth. If the shape of your original papier mâché is more complicated, you will have to think about making tucks and cuts in the paper to follow the contours, or you can think in terms of a design that has long thin projections easy to bend around corners. For example, if you are

making Christmas lanterns, you could cover them with foil-covered paper by cutting star-shapes with very long radiating rays (see Figure 63) and interlocking these rays over the surface.

Découpage is a technique like collage, in which you cut out pictures or patterns from magazines and newspapers and stick these over the surface of your papier mâché. Very amusing results can be obtained in this way, and the technique has been used very successfully for window displays and similar commercial display work. If, for example, you make up the shape of a head in paper, either as laminated papier mâché over a Plasticine mould, or just roughly constructed over a ball of pasted paper, you can cut out eyes, nose, mouth, and so on from newspaper pictures and advertisements and compose the features as you please. Surrealist effects can be obtained by using unexpected features or even entirely inappropriate cut-outs on a conventional papier mâché model. It is impossible to give directions for this kind of art: it depends entirely

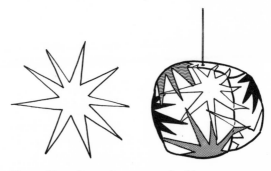

Figure 63. Paper box covered with cut-out stars.

on a kind of visual wit and the ability to recognise unusual combinations of shapes and pieces of a picture that go well together.

Papier mâché finished off with paper alone as the top layer needs to be protected against the damp. If your colours or print are rather fugitive, use one of the aerosol varnish sprays sold in art and craft stores for fixing water colours, chalk drawings, and so on. If the surface will stand it, copal or polyurethane clear varnish are tougher and more water-resistant. If you have any doubts about the paper you are using for the top surface, whether it is wallpaper or newspaper, take a small piece and coat it with the varnish you hope to use. If the colour or print do not run or fade, you can use the varnish safely on your model.

BASE PAINTS

If you intend to paint your papier mâché, you will need a priming coat of paint to cover irregularities in the appearance of the paper. Sometimes, even if you use white paper to finish off, the print from newspaper shows through in places, and in any case, even after sandpapering, the paper surface is never quite smooth.

White vinyl emulsion paint, ordinary household emulsion paint, is very suitable for this purpose, and you will find that two coats will cover almost any papier mâché with a smooth white surface on which to paint.

One of the main advantages of emulsion paint is that the surface takes almost any kind of paint — poster colour, oil paint, acrylic colours or even felt tip pens. If you want a slightly glossier finish, use the grades of emulsion paint designed to give an egg-shell gloss finish. Remember, however, that these are harder to paint on. Usually it is better to use ordinary matt emulsion paint and get the gloss by varnishing over the colours.

Gesso is a thicker kind of paint used extensively for covering matt surfaces. You can buy acrylic gesso that is very efficient as a covering medium for papier mâché and

can be thinned with gesso medium to get any degree of covering from a light whitening to a heavy ceramic-like finish.

If you wish, you can make gesso for yourself. Stir about half a pound of good smooth plaster of Paris into a gallon of cold water. Keep on stirring until after the usual setting time of the plaster — this is to make sure that it does not form any hard lumps — and then leave it overnight or longer. You should have a layer of clear water lying on top of a thick white mud of hydrated plaster.

Pour off the excess water, and add to the sludge of plaster half its volume of white (PVA) glue, stirring vigorously (a matter of necessity, the mixture will be very stiff). When the plaster is well distributed through the adhesive, stir in about an ounce of copal varnish or linseed oil and keep stirring until this has been dispersed in the mixture.

This will give you enough gesso to cover quite a large piece of work, such as the statues or stage scenery described in Chapter seven. If you need to keep it for another day, pour the excess into a polythene bag and clip the neck or opening tight to prevent the glue from drying.

You can find many recipes for gesso — every book of artists' formulae gives a different one. In essence they all consist of whiting or gypsum (hydrated plaster) mixed with glue of some sort and with the addition of linseed or other drying oils to make the glue more waterproof.

Be careful when using gesso that your paper mâché is quite dry before you apply the base paint. This is particularly important with papier mâché pulp work. If the paper still contains moisture, it will go on shrinking slightly longer after the gesso has set to a hard, brittle layer, and eventually the papier mâché will shrink away from the gesso and the gesso will flake off.

You can use poster colours on gesso, but they do not take as well as on emulsion paint. Acrylic colours are better for a gesso surface. Good gesso should last almost indefinitely — many fifteenth century altar pieces were painted on this material as a ground, and the colours are still firmly attached.

MARBLING

A very quick way of getting an attractive coloured pattern onto paper or papier mâché work is to marble it. The process requires very little skill, and anyone with a good eye for colour combinations can achieve really fine results.

You have probably seen the very fine marbled endpapers which were used in old books. These were made by spreading lines of colour over a deep tray full of fairly stiff gum tragacanth, almost in the form of a jelly, shaping these colours to the characteristic streaky patterns required with brass combs and similar tools, and then laying the sheets of paper over the surface of the gum so that they picked up the colour.

Now it is possible to get similar effects far more easily by spreading the colours, in a thin oil medium, over the surface of water in a bowl or pitcher, creating the streaky patterns by drawing a pencil or any other instrument through the lines of colour, and then dipping the object to be marbled right through the layer of colour into the water and then out again. The colours are picked up on the surface, and as soon as the water has dripped off they set in the marbled patterns.

You can buy colours specially made up in a thin oil medium for marbling work, and these are very efficient. If you want to make up your own, take ordinary oil colours in the transparent shades (Rose Madder, Viridian, and so on) and thin the paint with turpentine until you can drop it easily into water. It will float on the surface of the water in the form of an irregular ring or streak. Carry on dropping your other colours in the same way until you have all the contrast you need for your colour scheme: the spots of colour should not mix if you drop them carefully, but remain as a pattern of separate shades. Now draw a spatula, pencil, or any other thin hard object slowly through the surface of the water. The film of multi-coloured paint will

follow it, making a 'spiky' projection with various coloured fringes. Very often one or two movements of this kind will make an interesting pattern on top of the water, but in any case you will soon learn how to make a variety of shapes.

Dip in your papier mâché object – plate, bowl, animal model or whatever it is that you want to decorate – then draw it up again smoothly. If you want to marble the whole of an object you may have to fix a temporary handle to it – a large straight pin or something of that kind – to keep your fingers out of the paint.

As you draw it up, the model will pick up paint in a marbled pattern. Put it on a sheet of polythene to drip (although with luck no paint will come off it, only water) and leave it to dry. If your model has a hollow centre that can be reached, say through the money slit of a piggy bank, stop up this hole with Plasticine or similar material before you dip, otherwise the model will fill with water and may get broken down by the weight, especially as the papier mâché will be soft and soggy.

Marbling is of course a restricted way of decorating, depending as it does on the chance patterns into which the paint flows. However, you can soon learn to develop good colour schemes. A little black, preferably added in two or three small drops in different parts of the paint film, helps to give 'edge' to the marbling and makes the shapes less vague and bland. Often quite effective designs can be made with black and only one other colour. If you are interested in marbling, look at the end-papers of old books and the edges of the old-fashioned type of account book, and see how cleverly the workmen used to distribute the colours in this old craft.

GILDING

Many of the objects made with papier mâché lend themselves to elaborate Baroque or even Rococo design, and this style of decoration is often improved by gilding, especially on the highlights.

Traditional gilding is done with sheets of gold leaf, and this still remains the best way to obtain a completely permanent gold finish with a beautiful lustre. It is, let me say at once, rather difficult and rather expensive, but if you have made, say, a fine and elaborate mirror frame or candlestick in papier mâché, you may prefer to use the best in the way of decoration.

There are really five stages in the preparation of a properly gilded surface, although it is possible to combine one or two of the stages into one operation. First the background of the gilded area must be coloured a reddish-orange. This is because the metal leaf is very slightly transparent and the gilding has more 'body' if there is a gold-coloured paint to show through. Also there may be tiny gaps between pieces of the leaf, and again the paint hides these effectively.

Second, the area is prepared with a size which sticks the gold leaf down. Many of the sizes of former times were mixtures of egg white (known as 'glair' to the gilders) and glue, often mixed with a suitable reddish pigment so that the size did both of the first stages at once. You can buy very good materials sold as *gold size* at craft and art suppliers.

Alternatively you can make up a very good size for gold leaf with a mixture of Venice turpentine and beeswax (5 parts of beeswax and 1 part of Venice turpentine melted together). Warm the mixture before you apply it to your papier mâché and put it on with a small brush (unless you intend to gild a large area). If you cannot get hold of Venice turpentine, use a mixture of 5 parts beeswax, $\frac{3}{4}$ part spirits of turpentine, and $\frac{1}{4}$ part resin. The resin makes the mixture tacky so that it holds the metal leaf tightly.

The third stage of gilding is to lay the gold leaf onto the size. This requires great care. Gold leaf is very light and can blow about with a breath of wind, so do not work in a draught. To handle gold leaf, cut the edge of the book of leaves with a knife to release the sheets, and manoeuvre each sheet to the edge of a piece of flat wood which is your 'palette'. Professional gilders use a wood palette and a cushion covered with velvet that holds the leaves until ready, but for occasional gilding you can just have a smooth piece of wood. Cut the leaf to shape with a knife or scissors, and transfer it to the sized area by picking it up with the hairs of a water-colour brush dipped in alcohol or turpentine spirits. Don't let the brush get too wet: it should be just moist enough to hold the gold leaf for a moment or so.

The fourth stage is rubbing the leaf down and burnishing it to bring up the lustre. Rub the leaf down with a small piece of cotton wool (never touch leaf with your fingers: you will just become a small version of the Man with the Golden Arm), and burnish it with something hard and smooth. Professionals use special tools made of polished agate, but for a small job you can use the back of a stainless steel spoon.

The fifth and last stage, if you want the finest effect, is to give your gold a thin coating of varnish, preferably clear acrylic varnish slightly tinted with clear orange dye. You can buy such varnishes ready-made from some suppliers.

The cheaper alternative to gold leaf is a leaf made of a brass-type alloy called *Dutch metal*. The leaves resemble gold leaf, but are thicker and easier to handle. The technique is exactly the same as for gold leaf, except that it is *essential* to varnish Dutch metal gilding, otherwise it will discolour in a month or two.

If you do not want to go to the trouble of gilding with metal leaf, there are plenty of good metallic paints in various shades of gold – antique gold, green gold, and so on. These are, of course, very poor imitations of gold leaf, but will do very well for rough work or stage properties. If you are working for a stage with anywhere near the professional level of lighting, make sure to cover your gold paint with a thick layer of red to vermilion varnish. This looks entirely fake in daylight, but gives the authentic gleam of gold under stage lights. For work that is to be seen from close to, such as TV properties, you can compromise by painting the gilded parts in gold paint, and then, while the paint is still tacky, blow a little 'gold' powder over it. This powder is really anodised aluminium, but it looks good if it is in the upper layers of the paint. The real difficulty with gold paint is that the metal flakes tend to sink into the paint during drying — by blowing on a few on top of the paint layer you improve the lustre a great deal.

If you want an antique gold effect, gild the whole of an object with gold paint (don't be too elaborate, all the fine detail will be covered up), and then dab over a scumble of greenish-black paint in the hollows. Wipe it off the highlights with a piece of cloth while the paint is still wet.

VARNISHES AND FIXATIVES

Nearly all papier mâché work needs to be varnished to protect the paper and any painting on it from the damp. The only exceptions are those pieces of work that need so much protection that they are soaked in oil or paint all through.

Fixatives are the lightest type of varnish, and should be used if you want an almost matt effect. Many good fixatives are sold in art and craft stores — they are used to cover pastel drawings and water-colour paintings, etc. An aerosol spray pack is useful for applying light coats of fixative.

Alternatively, if you want to make up your own, dissolve one ounce of mastic or damar resin in a mixture of 12 oz (fluid) of gum turpentine and 12 oz of amyl acetate (cellulose thinners, banana oil). Do not use heat when dissolving the resin: both the solvents are highly inflammable.

Damar and *mastic resins* at a higher concentration give a varnish that will waterproof the surface of papier mâché and give a shiny finish. These varnishes can be purchased at art and craft stores or made up with a mixture of 1 oz of either of the resins to 1 oz each of gum turpentine and amyl acetate. The varnish has a slightly yellow tint.

Copal varnish is tougher than mastic or damar and will protect papier mâché very well. Buy the commercial varnish from a hardware store: it will be very much cheaper than the same material sold for artists' use.

Because all the natural resins tend to have a yellowish colour, and also may darken on exposure to light, I prefer to use the modern synthetic varnishes which are water-white. *Acrylic varnish* is very effective, but probably the best varnish for papier mâché is clear *polyurethane varnish*, which is clear, shiny, tough, and slightly flexible so that it stands up well to any slight shrinkage of the papier mâché after it has been applied. You can buy the varnish from household paint suppliers.

Epoxy resins can be useful for varnishing and strengthening papier mâché. These are the resins that are used in conjunction with glass fibre for building boats and car bodies, and for doing repairs. To prepare them, you have to mix a catalyst with the resin, which then turns from a fairly viscous liquid into a hard solid.

For a varnish, you should use the clear resin that is sold for embedding small objects for decoration. Mix it with the catalyst as directed by the supplier, and paint it over your model. This clear casting resin does not set very fast at room temperature, and you would be advised to place the varnished object on a radiator or in a warm cupboard for a day or so.

In one or two projects in this book I have recommended epoxy resin for reinforcing papier mâché from inside. In these cases you need not use the clear casting resin, you can use the rather opaque material that is sold for boat building and similar purposes. This sets much faster than the clear variety.

Finally, in emergency, you can make quite a good varnish from bits of scrap *polystyrene* (this is the clear, hard, rather brittle plastic that is used as a kind of glass substitute for many household articles, food boxes for the pantry, and so on). As these things tend to crack and break quite easily, most homes will have a supply of broken bits. You can also use polystyrene foam, Styrofoam, from ceiling tiles and packaging material, although you will find that it takes a lot of foam to make a little varnish.

Dissolve the polystyrene in amyl acetate: the simplest way to do this is to pack a jar with broken pieces of plastic and then pour in amyl acetate to about half way up the jar. Put a lid on to stop the solvent from evaporating, and leave it for a few days. This varnish is very clear but somewhat brittle, like the plastic it is made from. If you have difficulty in getting amyl acetate, some paint brush cleansers will work just as well — in the British market, for instance, Polyclens makes quite a good varnish with polystyrene and Imperial in the American.

When working with epoxy resin or polystyrene, brushes should be cleaned with acetone. Many suppliers of fibreglass materials sell this solvent as a brush cleanser. Always, when working with solvents of this kind, keep clear of fires and naked flames, and do not smoke while you are varnishing. Try to make sure that there is plenty of fresh air, as some of the solvents can make you dizzy in a confined space.

Suppliers

Papier mâché as a craft is most economical. Nearly all the materials you need can be found around the home, and you can produce very good work with nothing more than newspapers, wallpaper adhesive and household paints. For more complicated work, however, the following suppliers will be found useful.

ALLCRAFT, 11 Market Street, Watford, Hertfordshire. WD1 7AA (plaster, casting resin, paints).

HAMES, 32 Well Street, Paignton, Devonshire. TQ3 3AW (boxes for decorating).

LEISURECRAFTS, Romford Road, London E.12 (jewelry accessories).

POLYCELL PRODUCTS LTD., Broadwater Road, Welwyn Garden City, Hertfordshire. (adhesives and fillers). *

QUADRIGA PRODUCTS, 18 Rudds Lane, Haddenham, Buckinghamshire (adhesives, preservatives, varnishes).

STRAND GLASS CO. Ltd., 10 Haigh Avenue, Whitehill Industrial Estate, Stockport, Cheshire (epoxy resins, casting resins).

WESTBY PRODUCTS, School Lane, East Keswick, nr Leeds. LS17 9DA (casting resins, plaster).

All the paints and colours mentioned in this book can be obtained through art dealers from Reeves and Winsor and Newton.

*The Polytechniques Centre at this address can supply Polytechniques wall charts and Polycraft Project cards for school class use. These describe a number of craft uses for adhesives and fillers.

Index